# DON'T GET DERAILED BY YOUR ATTACHMENT STYLE

A STEP-BY-STEP APPROACH TO ADDRESS ANXIETY, WIN BACK CONFIDENCE, AND FEEL SECURE IN RELATIONSHIPS

LEIGH W. HART

401
—Publishing—

# CONTENTS

*Elevate your journey with.....*

# EXCLUSIVE COMPLIMENTARY SUPPORT MATERIALS!

## As a FREE Gift:

I have created a collection of **60+ journal pages and interactive worksheets** that perfectly complement the steps discussed in this book.

Simply go to:

## www.LeighWHart.com

to receive your FREE printable support materials.

# TRIGGER WARNING

# INTRODUCTION

---

*Try not to confuse attachment with love. Attachment is about fear and dependency and has more to do with love of self than love of another. Love without attachment is the purest love because it isn't about what others can give you because you're empty. It is about what you can give others because you're already full.*

— YASMIN MOGAHED

---

Are you stuck in a cycle of fear and self-doubt in your personal relationships? Have you ever wondered why you feel insecure or clingy in some relationships while feeling distant or avoidant in others? Well, at its core, it's about attachment styles. These attachment styles refer to the emotional connection we develop with others as a result of our early experiences with our caregivers.

Your dominant attachment style is formed early in your life and can impact the way you interact with others throughout your life. Unfortunately, when people develop an attachment disorder, it's challenging to establish and maintain healthy relationships.

They affect how we communicate, trust, and behave in romantic partnerships, friendships, and even in the workplace. As a social creature, building positive connections with others is essential for your well-being. However, if you have a fearful or disorganized attachment style, you might not feel safe in relationships or struggle to trust, while if your attachment style is avoidant, you might have difficulty allowing yourself to be vulnerable and connect with someone.

These traits can lead to a variety of problems, from feeling anxious and insecure in relationships to sabotaging them altogether. Nonetheless, by understanding your attachment style, you can recognize patterns of behavior that may hold you back from forming healthy, fulfilling relationships, which can ultimately lead to personal growth and development.

In this book, I will cover all four attachment styles because I recognize that some of you may not be familiar with your own attachment style yet, and it's possible that your current or future partner may have a different attachment style than you. So understanding all four styles will be beneficial now and in the future.

But how can you determine your attachment style? What are the different types of attachment styles, and how do they impact your relationships?

If you have an attachment disorder, you may commonly experience a lack of trust and struggle to feel safe and secure in your relationships. This difficulty can manifest as self-destructive behaviors, causing you to remain in a poor relationship or sabotaging your own efforts to find a healthy one. For instance, you may find yourself repeating the same dysfunctional patterns of interactions and feeling emotionally distant and afraid to let people in. Or, you may end up becoming dependent or overly clingy in relationships.

Unfortunately, this situation is not uncommon, and many people may relate to these struggles. However, it is essential to understand that having an attachment disorder does not mean that all hope is lost for building fulfilling relationships because it's possible to change your insecure attachment style! It doesn't have to be permanent. With determination and effort, you can cultivate a secure attachment style. While change isn't easy, you can learn how to break these negative cycles and create a secure, loving relationship with yourself and your partner.

And if you're not in a relationship, you're still in the right space. If you're struggling to connect to someone on the dating scene or you've noticed certain habits have played out in your past relationships, this could be a result of your attachment style—and the content within these chapters will help you break the cycle.

This book will be your guide every step of the way: From understanding what an attachment disorder is and how it affects your relationships (with your partner, friends, or family), to taking the necessary steps toward creating secure attachments. If you're in a relationship, you will have the tools to improve it, and if you're single, you'll be more prepared to enter a healthy relationship when the time is right.

To do so though, it is crucial to recognize how attachment styles can impact your life and seek the help necessary to overcome any obstacles you may encounter. For this reason, I decided to start the book with two relaxation sections instead of diving straight into the deep work.

Although this book is on attachment theory, before you dive into learning about this complex subject, it is important to create a basic foundation. So the first two chapters are designed to start you on the right path with two healthy ways to address any anxiety this healing journey creates. Not to mention, learning to journal and becoming proficient with breathing techniques will help you for years to come.

Overall, you must remember that you are not alone in your struggles, and getting help isn't a sign of weakness but rather a sign of strength and courage. By seeking help to build healthy relationships, you can live a fulfilling and meaningful life. If you are looking for a way to finally break free from your cycles of fear and self-doubt, then this book was written for you!

With *Don't Get Derailed by Your Attachment Style*, you will gain insight into yourself and your relationships. You will learn to recognize and process your emotions in a more healthy way, and you will gain the tools you need to build successful and satisfying relationships. In 17 steps, you can learn to build confidence in yourself and in your partner. So, if a specific step or topic especially resonates with you, I encourage you to explore that subject further. As you gain more self-awareness, you'll be able to identify areas that are more specific to your individual needs.

As for my story, it wasn't until later in life that attachment issues became a real problem. For the most part, I was a secure person until a series of traumatic events in my 30s changed everything. It wasn't until I sought help from a trained counselor that I was diagnosed with a severe anxiety disorder and post-traumatic stress disorder (PTSD). Because of my trauma, I slipped into an avoidant attachment style. It took me years to truly repair the damage caused by trauma, anxiety, and PTSD.

To overcome my past and truly heal, I took responsibility for my well-being. I made significant lifestyle changes, including counseling sessions, yoga and meditation practices, boundary setting, maintaining a healthy diet, extensive reading, and diligent self-reflection. And, because of my persistent efforts to heal, I finally regained the ability to form secure attachments in my life once again. So, I know personally that it *can* be done. Healing *is* possible, one step at a time!

With the right help, you too can overcome your past and create a better future. After reading this book, you will have:

- a better understanding of your attachment style
- improved communication skills
- growth in your self-confidence
- a more secure and healthy relationship with your partner
- a greater understanding of the power of self-love and acceptance

Throughout this book, there will be journal prompts and exercises for you to complete as you make your way through all the steps. Utilize your own journal or enhance your journey by going to www.LeighWHart.com, where you can receive complimentary customized journal pages and interactive worksheets specifically tailored to strengthen your experience with the steps outlined in this book. These valuable resources are thoughtfully designed to complement and amplify your progress as you delve deeper into the content.

Following the steps and advice in this book can empower you to break free from the chains of your insecure attachment style and create a more fulfilling relationship with yourself and your partner. There are many books online today about improving relationships, but this book is different because it focuses on not just the external factors but also the internal journey of getting to know yourself and building better connections.

By committing to the process outlined in this book, you are making a valuable investment in both yourself and your relationships. You deserve to be in a healthy, loving relationship, and with the help of this book, you can learn how to get there. So, if you are ready to take the next step and learn how to develop a secure attachment with your partner, let's get started!

# 1

# STEP 1: WRITE DOWN YOUR THOUGHTS

---

*Journal writing, when it becomes a ritual for transformation, is not only life-changing but life-expanding.*

— JEN WILLIAMSON

---

Have you ever felt like your thoughts were overwhelming and all-consuming? Like you have so much swirling around in your mind that it's hard to focus on anything else? This can be especially true for people with attachment anxiety or post-traumatic stress disorder (PTSD), who may experience racing thoughts, intrusive memories, or negative self-talk on a regular basis.

One powerful tool for managing these overwhelming thoughts is simply writing them down. By putting your thoughts on paper (or screen), you give them a tangible form outside of your own mind. This can help you see them more objectively and can even create a sense of distance or separation from them.

It can be intimidating to start writing, especially if you're not used to it or have had negative experiences with it in the past. But remember that there's no right or wrong way to do it. You can write in a journal, on scraps of paper, or even on your phone. You can write in complete sentences, fragments, or just jot down single words or phrases.

The important thing is that you're taking the time to acknowledge and process your thoughts in a way that works for you. These written thoughts will become key to understanding your attachment style, triggers, reactions, and eventual growth. By reviewing your thoughts, good or bad, and reflecting on them, you can gain insight into your feelings and their sources.

Creating an ongoing record of your thoughts is a valuable tool for gaining self-awareness and understanding of your attachment trauma. By the end of this chapter, you'll understand how to develop a regular writing practice that will help you gain insight into yourself, your attachment style, and your thoughts. So, grab your journal or downloaded worksheets, and let's begin!

## BENEFITS OF WRITING DOWN YOUR THOUGHTS

The plethora of benefits from journaling comes from the act of writing itself as well as from reflecting on what you wrote in the past. Writing can be a great way to express yourself and explore your thoughts and feelings. It can help you process difficult emotions and work through challenging situations.

One of the crucial benefits of journaling is having a simple record of your thoughts, experiences, and feelings. Journaling allows you to keep track of important events in your life, which can serve as a reminder of where you have been, what you have accomplished, and the intentional direction that you want to continue going in. This can be extremely helpful for creating goals and determining what steps need to be taken to achieve them.

Another significant advantage of journaling is that it helps clear your mind and assists in decision-making. When you write down your thoughts and feelings, you can review your emotions and why you feel a certain way. Then you can process those emotions and come to conclusions about what you want to do next. By writing out your options, you are better able to weigh the pros and cons, reducing stress and anxiety levels that may be affecting your ability to decide.

In a similar fashion, journaling helps to clarify emotions. Sometimes, it's challenging to articulate feelings and thoughts coherently, but writing them down can help you understand and comprehend them better. Writing can also help identify the cause of negative emotions, providing the opportunity to work through them and resolve them before they spiral out-of-control.

What's better about journaling is that it can help people tap inward and into the unknown. Your thoughts and feelings can provide insights into subconscious thoughts and emotions that may be buried deep beneath the surface. Journaling serves as an essential tool to get to know oneself better and gain a deeper understanding of one's desires, behaviors, and motivations.

Journaling can also prompt high-level thinking and awareness. When you sit down to write, it requires you to reflect on your experiences and think critically about your actions and choices. This allows you to develop a deeper understanding of who you are and how your actions impact others and yourself.

Probably one of the best perks of journaling is that it can offer a private space to reflect on uncomfortable or hurtful experiences. By writing down your painful history, you can process your emotions and work through the negative connotations associated with the event. It can also serve as a space to vent and express emotions that may be too difficult to express out loud.

Another amazing benefit of journaling is that you are the author of your own story. Through journaling, you get to tell your story on your terms, sharing and processing experiences as you see fit. This can be an empowering feeling and can provide a sense of control over one's life.

And in doing so, journaling can help you feel more accomplished by "completing" a goal or journal. Having a regular journaling habit can serve as a reminder of small successes and milestones accomplished along the way. Filling out your journal from front to back with entries can be a powerfully satisfying experience. This can serve as a great motivator to keep writing and maintain the habit.

Finally, journaling is a simple habit and routine to build upon. It is a low-stakes activity that you can do at any time or place, requiring nothing more than a pen and a piece of paper. It can also be modified to meet anyone's specific needs, making it a flexible habit.

Overall, the benefits of writing down your thoughts and feelings and having regular journaling habits are numerous. It is an effective tool to process emotions, and by making it a habit, individuals can experience these benefits while also managing stress, anxiety, and chronic PTSD symptoms.

## HOW TO CREATE A HABIT OF JOURNALING

Journaling and reviewing one's thoughts can be helpful practices for individuals dealing with attachment anxiety or PTSD. Here are some suggestions for making it a regular habit:

- Be creative with prompts: A major barrier to making journaling a regular practice is not knowing what to write about. An easy way to overcome this barrier is to use prompts. Prompts can be a single word or a question that encourages you to explore your thoughts and feelings. You can create a list of prompts that you can turn to when you're feeling stuck or use online resources for inspiration.

- Don't compare yourself to others: Journaling is a personal practice. Everyone's journaling process looks different, and there is no "proper" way to journal. You may find it helpful to share your writing with others, but it's important not to compare your writing to theirs. Instead, focus on your own thoughts and feelings and use writing as a tool for self-reflection.

- Set aside a realistic schedule to dedicate to journaling: Setting aside a specific time in your day or week to journal can be a helpful way to make it a regular habit. However, it's important to set a realistic timeframe that works for your schedule. It could be five minutes a day or an hour on the weekends. The most important thing is to find a schedule that works for you and stick to it.

## WHAT TO WRITE

Keeping a journal can be an effective, fun, and useful practice. It can help you process your emotions, keep track of your progress, and set goals for the future. In order to get the most out of journaling, there are a few key practices to consider. Here are some tips on what to include in your journal:

- Record and celebrate your accomplishments: Write down your achievements. This will help you recognize your progress and give you a sense of accomplishment. It's important to celebrate big and small accomplishments as they come. It's helpful to categorize and date your accomplishments.
- Review your daily experiences: Reflect on your daily experiences, both good and bad. Write in detail about what happened and how you felt. Consider what you learned from each experience.
- Collect quotes: Collect inspiring quotes that resonate with you. Write them down in your journal. You can refer to these quotes when you need a little extra motivation or inspiration.
- Use the space to create, review, and maintain your goals: Use your journal to set and track your goals. Write them down, create milestones, and check-in regularly to see how you're progressing. Regularly

reflecting on your goals will help you stay focused and motivated.

- Practice gratitude: Write down things you are grateful for. This can be a powerful practice that can improve your mood and give you perspective.
- Create a "Let-it-go" list: Write down things that are bothering you on your "Let-it-go" list. This can include negative emotions, worries, or anything else that is troubling you. Once you've written it down, set it aside, and let-it-go.
- Make a bucket list: Create a list of things you want to do and experience in your lifetime. This can be a fun and inspiring way to dream big and stay motivated.
- Create your five- or ten-year plan: Think about where you want to be in five or ten years. Write down your goals and create a plan to achieve them.
- Use prompts to address your inner child's healing: Inner child healing can be a powerful practice. Use journal prompts to explore this process and connect with your inner child.

By including the practices outlined above, you can make journaling a helpful tool in your journey toward healing and personal growth.

## JOURNAL PROMPTS

Sprinkled throughout some chapters are journal prompts. You are free to use your own journal to reflect on these questions or go to www.LeighWHart.com to download free customized journal pages and worksheets.

Write down any goals or intentions you may have. Since you're only beginning, you can create more vague goals like "I want to have a healthy relationship with my partner" or "I want to feel more organized." As you go along your journey, refer to this prompt often and make it more specific, such as "I want to speak to my partner without raising my voice" or "I want to take 10 minutes every morning to meditate."

Each time you return, reassess your goals and intentions to see how far you have come:

- The "let-it-go" list. A let-it-go list is a list of things that you need to let go of in order to move forward. These can be past traumas, disappointments, feelings of self-doubt, etc. Write down every worry or negative emotion you are experiencing and take the time to process it. Once you have taken the time to reflect on each item, cross them out one by one and release the negative emotions connected with them.
- Now that you have created a list of what you would like to let go of, create a list of healthy emotions you would like to experience and brainstorm ways to

make that happen. For example, if you want to feel more joy or enthusiasm in your life, what small steps can you take toward achieving that? Can you spend some time outdoors, take a dance class, or call an old friend? Write down these ideas and use them to fuel your intentions. These will also come in handy in Step 12.

- In this chapter, we reviewed a variety of methods that you can use to improve your journaling and emotional experience. For example, you can practice gratitude, reflect on your feelings for the day, or record your accomplishments. Each day, pick 2–3 prompts and complete them. Make this a regular habit and track your progress over time. Remember, the goal is to be open and honest with yourself in order to gain insight and clarity into your emotions.

As you can see, a simple habit like writing down your thoughts in a journal can be incredibly powerful. Give yourself the gift of time, space, and creativity to express your thoughts and feelings while embracing your healing journey. In the meantime, we'll review another popular relaxation technique: breathing.

# 2

# STEP 2: WHEN ANXIETY KEEPS YOU COMPANY... BREATHE

*Breathe deeply, until sweet air extinguishes the burn of fear in your lungs and every breath is a beautiful refusal to become anything less than infinite.*

— D. ANTOINETTE FOY

Breathing is one of the most instinctive yet overlooked abilities we possess as humans. You breathe without even thinking about it, but have you ever stopped and paid attention to your breath? This book may stir up some feelings, so before proceeding, this chapter will prepare you with breathing techniques you can use for sudden anxiety attacks now and during your healing journey. And if that situation arises, remember to apply some of the journaling strategies from Step 1 to document the emotions and thoughts that preceded your panic attack.

Deep breathing exercises have been proven to alleviate symptoms of anxiety and PTSD. When you're feeling anxious or stressed, your breath becomes shallow and rapid, which in turn creates more tension in your body. By focusing on deep breathing techniques, you can tap into your parasympathetic nervous system, which helps you relax and reduce stress levels. So, let's take a deep breath together and explore the power of our breath.

## BENEFITS OF BREATHING EXERCISES

Breathing exercises are a simple yet powerful way to improve both physical and mental health. They involve breathing patterns that promote relaxation, reduce stress and anxiety, increase mindfulness and focus, and can even help with sleep disorders. Breathing techniques can be implemented in a creative and easy way for you to incorporate into your daily routine.

Deep breathing is an excellent way to enhance mental health, and it has immediate effects on stress, mood, and conscientiousness. Slow, deep breathing induces relaxation and helps reduce stress, anxiety, and depression. It promotes social connectedness by helping people communicate more effectively with others and express themselves more fully.

Breathing exercises can improve anxiety and overthinking, helping people feel more grounded and focused. They have been shown to help you relax and reduce anxiety levels, which can also help with improving sleep patterns. Practicing mindfulness meditation techniques is another great way to strengthen concentration and reduce anxiety.

Different emotions are associated with different breathing patterns, and changing how you breathe can change how you feel. Researchers have found that slow and deep breathing helps reduce negative emotions, such as anger, fear, and anxiety, while improving positive emotions, such as happiness, joy, and contentment. Breathing can provide a way to control and release pent-up emotions and help people feel more in control.

Breathing exercises can help people with PTSD manage their symptoms, such as flashbacks, intrusive thoughts, and hyperarousal. PTSD often involves having a heightened response to certain triggers, leading to intense anxiety and panic. By practicing breathing exercises that promote calmness and relaxation, people with PTSD can develop coping mechanisms to manage their symptoms more easily.

Ultimately, breathing exercises are a highly effective way to improve mental and physical well-being. Incorporating breathing exercises into a daily routine is easy, flexible, and accessible to everyone. By practicing these methods, individuals can take control of their well-being and improve their quality of life.

## TIPS AND TRICKS FOR THE BEST BREATHING TECHNIQUES

Breathing is a vital function that supports your body in numerous ways, including calming your mind and reducing anxiety and stress. Improving breath techniques is essential for individuals with anxiety or PTSD, as it can enhance feelings of relaxation and support mental well-being. Here are some tips to improve your breathing technique:

- Fill your belly: When breathing in, try to expand your belly or diaphragm, allowing your lungs to receive oxygen deeply. This technique is known as "belly breathing" or "diaphragmatic breathing." By focusing on filling your belly instead of your chest, you can improve the quality of your breathing and reduce feelings of anxiety.
- Have longer exhales: Breathing out for longer periods than inhaling can stimulate the vagus nerve, which helps regulate our parasympathetic nervous system, reducing stress and anxiety. Start by inhaling slowly through your nose and then exhaling through your mouth for twice as long. This technique can decrease your heart rate and increase your relaxation response.
- Focus on the breath and its feeling in your body: Pay attention to your breath and its sensations in your body. Concentrate on each inhale and exhale,

focusing on the quality of your breath. This helps to reduce anxious thoughts and can help you bring your attention to the present moment.

- Practice with various counts and breathing sounds: Experiment with different breathing cadences and styles. You can try inhaling for four counts, holding for two counts, and then exhaling for six counts. Use guided audio tracks, such as ocean wave sounds or forest ambiance, to cultivate a relaxation response.

Practicing these breathing techniques can improve your mental and physical well-being, reduce stress and anxiety, and bring a sense of calm to your mind and body. Take a few minutes every day to practice these techniques, and you will start feeling the benefits in no time.

## TYPES OF BREATHING EXERCISES FOR ANXIETY

Deep breathing techniques have been known to help individuals manage anxiety and PTSD symptoms. Here are some examples of effective deep breathing techniques:

- Lion's breath: Sit comfortably with your legs crossed and place your hands on your knees. Inhale deeply through your nose, then open your mouth and forcefully exhale while sticking out your tongue as far as possible. This breath can be repeated several times to release tension in the face and throat.

- The 4-7-8 breathing method: Close your mouth and inhale quietly through your nose for 4 seconds. Hold your breath for 7 seconds, then exhale through your mouth while making a whooshing sound for 8 seconds. This technique can be repeated up to four times in a row.

- The 4-1-7 breathing method: Breathe in through your nose for 4 seconds, hold your breath for 1 second, and exhale slowly through your mouth for 7 seconds. Repeat as often as needed to calm both the body and mind.

- The 3-4 breathing exercise: This exercise involves inhaling for 3 seconds and exhaling for 4 seconds. This can be done in a comfortable seated position while focusing on the breath.

- Box breathing: This technique is based on the idea of creating a box shape with your breaths. Breathe in for 4 seconds, hold for 4 seconds, exhale for 4 seconds, and hold for 4 seconds. You can repeat this several times, and it can be done anywhere, anytime.

- Alternate nostril breathing: Relax in a comfortable seated position and bring your right hand up to your face. Use your thumb to close off your right nostril and inhale through your left nostril for 3 seconds. Hold your breath for 1 second, then use your ring finger to close off your left nostril and exhale through your right nostril for 3 seconds. Repeat, alternating, until you feel better.

These deep breathing techniques can be powerful tools for individuals experiencing anxiety or PTSD symptoms. Practicing them regularly can bring a sense of calm and relaxation to the mind and body. So go ahead, take a deep breath, and give these techniques a try!

### Breathing Challenge

Before you proceed to the next chapter, I have a challenge for you. Take a moment to assess how you currently feel. How is your heart beating? How does your body feel? Then apply and perform at least one breathing exercise from the information above, and once you've completed the exercise, answer the following reflection questions.

- How do you feel after doing the exercise?
- Do you notice any differences in your body after the exercise?
- Did it help you calm your thoughts?

Remember, air and our breathing habits are vital for our well-being. Taking time each day to practice your breathing techniques can have a profound impact on your mental and physical health. Using these techniques, especially during an anxiety attack or other stressful moments, can be an effective tool to bring back a sense of calm and balance. Just take a few minutes each day to practice these breathing exercises, and you will start to reap the benefits in no time.

Once you've gotten comfortable embracing these techniques, you can move on to more self-reflective breath practices like meditation, which can further enhance your mental health. However, now that you have a few tools to help you manage some uncomfortable emotions, it's time to begin exploring the roots of human connection.

# 3

# STEP 3: UNDERSTANDING ATTACHMENT THEORY — EXPLORING THE ROOTS OF HUMAN CONNECTION

*Attachment is a deep and enduring emotional bond that connects one person to another person across time and space.*

— AINSWORTH

In this step, you will learn about attachment theory and the four types of attachments. I encourage you to follow along and determine if any of the information resonates with you and if you can identify your attachment style. At the end of step 4, you will take a quick quiz to see if you were right.

## WHAT IS ATTACHMENT THEORY?

Attachment theory refers to a psychological concept that explains how early childhood experiences with caregivers shape our ability to form healthy relationships later in life.

The history of attachment theory goes back to the mid-20th century when British psychologist John Bowlby began conducting research on the emotional bonds between babies and their caregivers. He observed that infants who were separated from their mothers for extended periods showed signs of distress, such as crying and agitation, even after being fed and changed.

Bowlby theorized, based on his research, that infants form attachments to their caregivers in order to fulfill their basic needs for safety, comfort, and security. These attachments, in turn, serve as a foundation for future social and emotional development. Bowlby's work gave rise to the concept of the "attachment bond," which refers to the close emotional connection between a child and their primary caregiver.

Attachment theory is developed through a process called "attachment styles," which refers to how children learn to interact with their caregivers. There are four primary attachment styles: anxious, avoidant, fearful or disorganized, and secure. Children who form secure attachments with their primary caregiver are likely to grow up feeling comfortable with intimacy and forming close relationships with others.

Those who form anxious attachments often feel insecure in relationships and may cling to their partners or worry about being abandoned. Children with avoidant attachments may avoid emotional closeness and have difficulty trusting others. The fearful or disorganized attachment style typically arises in response to abusive or neglectful caregivers and may lead to emotional and behavioral problems in adulthood.

As adults, our attachment style can have a significant impact on our relationships and overall well-being. Understanding our attachment style can help us recognize patterns in our behavior and work toward developing healthier relationships. For individuals with anxiety or PTSD, attachment theory may provide insights into the underlying causes of their symptoms and offer a roadmap for healing.

### *Stages of Attachment*

Attachment is the emotional bond that develops between a child and their primary caregiver. It is a crucial aspect of healthy emotional and social development. The stages of attachment can be broken down into four major categories: pre-attachment, indiscriminate attachment, discriminate attachment, and multiple attachments.

### Pre-Attachment

This stage of attachment occurs during the first few months of life, from birth to around six weeks. During this time, infants develop an awareness of their surroundings, including their caregivers. They have not yet formed a specific attachment to one individual but are beginning to recognize familiar faces and voices.

## Indiscriminate Attachment

From six weeks to seven months, infants begin to develop indiscriminate attachments. During this stage, infants will smile and show interest in anyone who gives them attention. They do not yet show a preference for one person over another.

## Discriminate Attachment

From seven months to one year, infants begin to form discriminating attachments. During this stage, infants will start to show a preference for familiar faces and voices. They may become shy or anxious around strangers and seek comfort from specific individuals, typically their primary caregiver.

## Multiple Attachments

After one year, infants begin to form multiple attachments with other individuals who provide them with consistent care and support. These may include grandparents, siblings, and other caregivers.

### *Factors That Influence Attachment*

Two significant factors influence the development of attachment: Opportunity for attachment and quality caregiving.

- Opportunity for attachment refers to the amount of time an infant spends with their primary caregiver. Infants who have consistent and frequent contact with their caregiver have a greater likelihood of forming a secure attachment.
- Quality caregiving involves the caregiver's responsiveness, sensitivity, and warmth toward the infant. Caregivers who are consistently attuned to their infant's needs and provide comfort and support when necessary, creates a secure attachment.

## ATTACHMENT STYLES

Attachment theory, developed by psychologist John Bowlby, suggests that infants form attachment bonds with their caregivers that lay the foundation for their future relationships. These attachment styles can influence how we approach relationships as adults. There are four types of attachment styles: anxious, avoidant, fearful or disorganized, and secure. Out of these four styles, secure attachment is the ultimate goal we all aspire to achieve. However, if we do not naturally embody a secure attachment style, we may find ourselves in one of the insecure styles: anxious, avoidant, or fearful or disorganized. Let's dive into each one and explore their characteristics and how they may affect you.

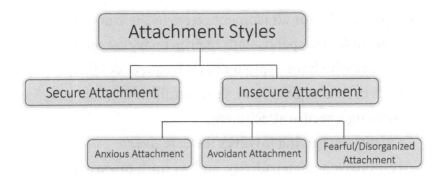

### Signs of Anxious Attachment

People with an anxious attachment style are often described as clingy or needy in relationships. They worry about their partner leaving or rejecting them and may become overly preoccupied with their relationship. They may seek constant reassurance from their partner to alleviate their anxiety and may become jealous or possessive. In essence, the person feels as if they are not enough and depends on their partner to validate their self-worth. As it relates to PTSD, individuals with an anxious attachment may struggle with trust issues, hyper-arousal responses, recurrent nightmares, and flash-backs following a traumatic event or trigger.

Example: Jane is in a relationship with Tom. Jane knows Tom loves her, but she still worries about him leaving her. Jane constantly expresses her love for Tom, seeking valida-tion and reassurance from him. When Tom spends time with his friends or at work, Jane may become anxious, fearing that he may prefer those people over her. As it relates to PTSD, Jane may have experienced childhood abandonment or neglect, which may have caused her to develop this anxious attachment style.

### Signs of Avoidant Attachment

A person with an avoidant attachment style tends to be emotionally distant and may avoid getting too close to others. They may appear independent and self-reliant, and they may suppress their emotions to avoid vulnerability. They may feel that relationships are a source of fear or that it is safer to remain single. As it relates to PTSD, individuals with an avoidant attachment may present with emotional numbing, limited social support, and detached affect following a traumatic event or trigger.

Example: Tim is in a relationship with Sophia. Tim struggles to tolerate intimacy and avoids telling Sophia how he feels. He may push her away when she tries to get emotionally close to him. When Sophia expresses her love, Tim may become uncomfortable or try to change the conversation. As it relates to PTSD, Tim may have experienced a traumatic event that severely impacted his ability to trust others, and he may feel safer keeping relationships at arm's length.

### Signs of Fearful or Disorganized Attachment

People with a fearful or disorganized attachment style may experience extreme anxiety in relationships. They may have experienced trauma early in life or had a caregiver who was inconsistent or abusive. Individuals with this attachment style may fear intimacy or relationships, but they also fear the idea of being alone. The internal conflict of wanting and needing relationships but fearing them can cause difficulties, such as chaotic relationships or frequent breakups. As related to PTSD, individuals with this attachment style may present with dissociation symptoms, flashbacks, and impaired reality testing.

*Example*: Lisa is in a relationship with Mark. Whenever she feels close to Mark, Lisa becomes fearful and may push him away or become clingy. If Mark tries to reassure Lisa or provide comfort, she may become anxious, fearing that he will leave her. As it relates to PTSD, Lisa may have experienced neglect, abuse, or violence in the past, causing her to feel unsafe and develop this fearful attachment style.

### Signs of Secure Attachment

People with a secure attachment style feel comfortable with intimacy and closeness in their relationships. They trust others and have a positive view of themselves and their partners. People with this attachment style can relate to others with ease and have healthy boundaries. They feel free to express their needs and emotions and can enjoy a relationship without fear of rejection or abandonment. As it relates to PTSD, individuals with a secure attachment may have had strong support systems following trauma or may have experienced minimal negative life events.

*Example*: Joe is in a relationship with Kacey. Joe feels comfortable with his relationship with Kacey and trusts that she loves him. He accepts her emotionally and physically without fear of rejection. Joe appreciates spending time with Kacey but also values their independence. As it relates to PTSD, Joe has never experienced a substantial traumatic event and has always had secure attachment relationships, which reflect his current attachment style.

Overall, understanding your attachment style can help you work through relationship difficulties and improve your ability to connect with others. Seek professional help if you find it difficult to handle your attachment issues.

## IMPACT OF EARLY ATTACHMENT

Early attachment plays a crucial role in shaping our lives as we grow older. It refers to the bond between a child and their primary caregiver, usually the mother. Studies have shown that the quality of attachment a child develops in their early years can have a profound impact on their emotional, mental, and social development.

Children who form secure attachments to their caregivers have stronger self-esteem, self-reliance, and independence. This means that they are more confident in their abilities and are better equipped to handle challenges and setbacks. They are also more likely to develop successful social relationships and perform well academically.

In contrast, children who have insecure attachments with their caregivers may develop a range of emotional and psychological issues, including depression, anxiety, and low self-esteem. These children may have difficulty forming healthy relationships with others and may struggle with academic achievement and general well-being.

It is important to note that early attachment is not a fixed trait and can be modified through interventions like therapy or counseling. Parents who are aware of the importance of attachment can take steps to promote a secure bond with their child. This can include giving their child consistent love and attention, responding promptly and sensitively to their needs, and ensuring a safe and nurturing environment.

Overall, the impact of early attachment cannot be overstated. By cultivating a strong bond with their caregivers, children can develop the tools they need to thrive emotionally, socially, and academically. This is especially important for individuals with anxiety or PTSD who may have experienced trauma or disruptions in early attachment. By understanding the importance of attachment and seeking professional help when necessary, individuals can work toward building healthier relationships and finding greater peace and happiness in their lives.

### Childhood Attachment Disorders

Attachment disorder is a serious psychiatric condition that occurs when a child or infant cannot develop healthy and secure relationships with caregivers. There are two distinct types of attachment disorders: Disinhibited Social

Engagement Disorder (DSED) and Reactive Attachment Disorder (RAD).

Disinhibited social engagement disorder occurs when a child shows overly friendly behavior with almost anyone, including strangers or untrustworthy individuals. This disorder often occurs in children who have been exposed to ongoing neglect, abuse, or inconsistent parenting. These children may display a lack of caution around people they don't know, hug or cuddle with them, and even accept gifts or food from them despite not knowing them well. This lack of social boundaries can make them vulnerable to abuse and exploitation, leading to future distress and trauma.

Reactive attachment disorder, on the other hand, occurs when a child cannot form healthy attachments with their primary caregivers, making it difficult for them to trust or bond with anyone else. These children rarely show any interest in forming relationships, either with their peers or new adults. They can be emotionally withdrawn, avoid physical touch, have difficulty comforting or being comforted, and often display extreme sadness and rage. The disorder is usually the result of neglect, traumatic separation, or abuse during an early part of their lives, such as infancy or the first few years of life.

Both DSED and RAD can have severe emotional and physical consequences, including depression, anxiety, post-traumatic stress disorder, and developmental disorders. Children with these disorders may feel conflicted, anxious, or experience an outburst of emotions when placed in new situations. They may also have trouble establishing positive relationships, leading to trouble at school or in social settings.

Some common challenges or complications include:

- difficulty trusting others
- difficulty forming secure attachments
- ongoing feelings of sadness and despair
- discomfort in social situations
- difficulty controlling emotions
- lack of progress in therapy and treatment

## JOURNAL PROMPTS

- Reflect on your childhood relationships and how they may have shaped your attachment style.
- Write down any memories, thoughts, and/or feelings you may have about your primary caregiver as a child.
- Think about your earliest memories of attachment-related experiences, such as interactions with primary caregivers or significant relationships during childhood. How do you recall feeling during those moments?
- What impact do you think those experiences have had on your attachment style?

- Think of a time when you felt safe and connected in a relationship. What were the underlying feelings that allowed you to experience this connection?
- Think of a time when you felt scared and disconnected in a relationship. Why do you think you felt this way?

As you can see, your dominant attachment style is developed in childhood, but its effects last well into adulthood, which we will review in Step 6. Luckily, you can improve and change your style. Now that you know the roots and basis of attachment theory, it's time to discover what your attachment style is.

# 4

# STEP 4: WHAT'S YOUR ATTACHMENT STYLE?

*I lived in misery, like every man whose soul is tethered by the love of things that cannot last and then is agonized to lose them.*

— ST. AUGUSTINE

Attachment is a critical component of human development, and it influences a person's emotions, relationships, and behaviors throughout their life. However, when something goes wrong with attachment, it can cause chaos and turmoil in a person's life. To understand yourself better, let's take a look at each attachment style and see which one resonates with you the most.

## ANXIOUS ATTACHMENT

Anxious attachment is a common emotional state that affects both men and women. It is a state of emotional insecurity that arises when you feel that your relationship with your partner is threatened or at risk of ending. Anxious attachment can be caused by several factors, such as early childhood experiences, previous negative relationships, or even genetics.

If you have an anxious attachment style, you tend to feel insecure in your relationships, frequently experiencing feelings of anxiety, jealousy, and fear of abandonment. You may often have a strong need for reassurance and validation from your partner and may become overly clingy or possessive. You may also have difficulty trusting your partner and often interpret their actions negatively.

The signs of anxious attachment can vary from one person to another, but some of the most common symptoms include:

- rapid heartbeat or racing thoughts in response to perceived danger
- difficulty sleeping, nightmares, or frequent awakenings
- low self-esteem and self-doubt
- negative self-talk and worry
- fear of rejection, abandonment, or being alone

- overly dependent on a partner for emotional support and validation

The effects of an anxious attachment style on adult relationships can be damaging and long-lasting. If you have this attachment type, you may frequently experience conflict in your relationships or avoid them entirely. You may become controlling or codependent, which can strain the relationship and cause your partner to feel trapped or suffocated. Over time, this can result in feelings of resentment, dissatisfaction, and emotional pain.

### Christine's Anxious Attachment

Christine, a 32-year-old woman, exhibits an anxious attachment style. In Christine's case, her anxious attachment style can be traced back to her upbringing. During childhood, Christine experienced inconsistent emotional support from her parents, which created an unpredictable environment for her to grow up in. Her parents' inconsistency in their emotional support made Christine feel like she never knew when she could count on them, which led her to develop a sense of uncertainty and anxiety in her interpersonal relationships.

As an adult, Christine's attachment style has influenced her behavior in several ways. For instance, she often feels anxiety when her partner seems distant or unavailable, and she's consumed by thoughts of being left alone. This fear of abandonment often results in her being clingy or too dependent on her partner. She constantly seeks reassurance from her partner, which can be exhausting for both of them.

In past relationships, Christine's anxious attachment style has led to several problems. In one instance, she became so concerned with her partner's well-being that she began to disregard her own needs. Christine did everything she could to make her partner happy because she was afraid of being alone, to the extent that she suffered from burnout. This type of behavior can ultimately push partners away and cause more harm than good in a relationship.

In another scenario, Christine's anxiety led her to become jealous and possessive of her partner. This type of behavior can be damaging to a relationship and can make partners feel overwhelmed and trapped.

### Anxious Attachment Quiz

Do you think you have an anxious attachment style? Below are ten yes-or-no questions. Answer honestly, and keep track of how many yes or no responses you have at the end.

| | Yes | No |
|---|---|---|
| Do you constantly seek reassurance from your romantic partner? | | |
| Do you often feel worried about your partner leaving you? | | |
| Do you have difficulty opening up to friends and family about your emotions? | | |
| Do you find yourself feeling jealous or possessive of your partner? | | |
| Do you experience feelings of anxiety or panic when your partner is not available? | | |
| Do you have a tendency to cling to your partner or become overly dependent on them? | | |
| Do you feel you cannot fully trust your partner? | | |
| Do you excessively apologize or apologize for things that are not your fault? | | |
| Do you have a fear of being abandoned or left alone? | | |
| Do you have difficulty maintaining healthy boundaries in your relationships? | | |

Scoring: If you answered yes to five or more questions, you may have an anxious attachment style. This means you are more likely to become overly dependent on others, have difficulty trusting your partner, and be overly sensitive to potential signs of rejection. As with any quiz or self-assessment, it's important to keep in mind that this is not a diagnosis, and it's always best to seek professional help if you have concerns about your attachment style and how it's affecting your relationships.

## AVOIDANT ATTACHMENT

Avoidant attachment is an emotional state that arises when a person feels that their relationship with their partner is threatened or at risk of ending. Avoidant attachment is characterized by a fear of becoming close to others, a lack of trust in relationships, and difficulty with intimacy.

If you have an avoidant attachment style, you may be emotionally distant and self-reliant, often avoiding any kind of long-term commitment or emotional investment in relationships. The signs of avoidant attachment can vary from one person to another, but some of the most common symptoms include:

- an unwillingness to open up and share feelings with others
- a fear of commitment or intimacy
- a need for control in relationships
- avoidance of emotional closeness or emotional expression
- trouble forming deep emotional connections with others

The effects that avoidant attachment styles have on adult relationships can be destructive. If you have this attachment type, you may find it difficult to trust and connect with your partner, often leading to feelings of resentment and alienation in the relationship. You may also struggle to commit or express love toward your partner due to a fear of getting hurt or rejected. Over time, these issues can cause communication problems, dissatisfaction, and even the dissolution of your relationship.

*Jack's Avoidant Attachment*

Jack, a 40-year-old man, exhibits an avoidant attachment style in his relationships. This attachment style is due to the past traumas he has experienced in life, especially in his early childhood. As a child, Jack was left alone and ignored by his parents, causing him to feel unimportant and unwanted.

In his current relationships, Jack is emotionally distant and often withdraws when things get too close or intimate. For instance, whenever his partner expresses their love or tries to connect with him emotionally, Jack will naturally shut down and create a physical and emotional distance. He prefers to keep his emotions hidden, and he refrains from sharing any personal matters with his partner.

Additionally, Jack tends to avoid commitment in relationships because he sees it as a vulnerability that could expose him to possible heartbreak. He will often end relationships before things get too serious as a way to protect himself from getting hurt.

Jack may appear to be uninterested in others or may be seen as arrogant, self-centered, or aloof. He may not feel comfortable in social settings or expressing emotions, leading others to view him as detached or unemotional.

As you can see, the avoidant attachment style displayed by Jack is an adaptation to overcome his early traumas. However, it has affected his ability to form and maintain healthy relationships, leading to emotional distance, commitment issues, and difficulty expressing emotions. With time, patience, and proper therapy, individuals with avoidant attachment styles can create more substantial and intimate relationships, and Jack is no exception.

### Avoidant Attachment Quiz

This quiz contains ten simple yes-or-no questions designed to help you determine if you have an avoidant attachment style.

Please answer the following questions as honestly as possible:

| | Yes | No |
|---|---|---|
| Do you find it difficult to express your emotions to others? | | |
| Do you often keep your problems to yourself instead of reaching out for help? | | |
| Do you feel uncomfortable when others get too emotionally close to you? | | |
| Do you tend to distance yourself from others when you feel overwhelmed or anxious? | | |
| Do you avoid intimacy and commitment in romantic relationships? | | |
| Do you often feel like you don't need others to be happy or fulfilled? | | |
| Do you feel like you have trouble trusting others, even those closest to you? | | |
| Do you have a tendency to shut down emotionally during conflicts? | | |
| Are you hesitant to rely on others for support or assistance? | | |
| Do you tend to avoid deep emotional conversations with others? | | |

Scoring: If you answered yes to four or more of these questions, there is a likelihood that you have an avoidant attachment style. This means that you tend to keep others at arm's length in order to protect yourself from emotional pain or vulnerability. You may struggle with intimacy and commitment in relationships and have difficulty trusting others.

## FEARFUL OR DISORGANIZED ATTACHMENT

Fearful or disorganized attachment is an emotional state characterized by a lack of trust in relationships, difficulty forming secure attachments with others, and an inability to regulate emotions. With this style, you will go back and forth between anxious and avoidant behaviors. In one moment, you are pushing your partner away. Then, in the next, you become clingy and possessive.

If you have this attachment style, you may often feel overwhelmed or confused when it comes to forming close relationships, leading you to become emotionally distant or avoidant. The signs of fearful or disorganized attachment can vary from one person to another, but some of the most common symptoms include:

- intense fear of being hurt or rejected
- difficulty forming and maintaining secure relationships
- inability to regulate emotions effectively
- confusion or ambivalence in relationships
- anxiety, depression, or other mental health issues

The effects that a fearful or disorganized attachment style has on adult relationships can be devastating. If you have this attachment type, you may find it difficult to trust or connect with your partner, often leading to feelings of insecurity and confusion in the relationship. You may also find it hard to show your partner how much you love them because you're afraid of hurting them or being turned down. This can lead to issues like communication problems, difficulty forming secure attachments, and even the dissolution of your relationship.

### Paul's Fearful or Disorganized Attachment

Paul is a 45-year-old man who struggles with a fearful or disorganized attachment style. Paul's attachment style can be traced back to his childhood traumas, where he experienced inconsistent and unpredictable behavior from his parents. They would sometimes be loving and affectionate, but other times, they would be emotionally or physically abusive toward him. These traumatic experiences left Paul feeling confused, anxious, and on edge, making it difficult for him to form secure attachments with others.

As a result, Paul's disorganized attachment style has affected his relationships in multiple ways. For example, when he is in a romantic relationship, he may initially appear clingy and overly dependent, desperately seeking reassurance and attention from his partner. However, as the relationship progresses, he may begin to push his partner away or become distant and avoidant, fearing that they will eventually leave him.

In platonic relationships, Paul may struggle to trust others or share personal information with them, fearing that they will use it against him. He may also have difficulty setting boundaries or asserting himself, as he constantly worries about upsetting or angering others.

### Fearful or Disorganized Attachment Quiz

Do you think you have a fearful or disorganized attachment style? Take this quiz to explore your attachment style and discover valuable insights into your relationship patterns.

|  | Yes | No |
|---|---|---|
| Do you avoid intimacy because it makes you uncomfortable? |  |  |
| Do you tend to keep your distance from others for fear of being rejected or hurt? |  |  |
| Do you ever find yourself feeling jealous or possessive in your relationships? |  |  |
| Do you frequently seek reassurance or validation from your partner? |  |  |
| Do you ever find yourself pushing your partner away, only to pull them back in moments later? |  |  |
| Do you feel like you struggle to communicate your emotions effectively with your partner? |  |  |
| Do you ever feel like you are overly dependent on your partner for emotional support? |  |  |
| Do you ever find yourself feeling confused or uncertain about your feelings toward your partner? |  |  |
| Do you have a habit of engaging in self-sabotaging behaviors in your relationships? |  |  |
| Do you ever find yourself feeling stuck in unsatisfying or unfulfilling relationships? |  |  |

Scoring: If you answered "yes" to more than half of these questions, you may have a fearful or disorganized attachment style. This means that you often feel anxious or uncertain in close relationships and struggle to build secure connections with your partner. You may find yourself feeling insecure, jealous, clingy, or dependent on your partner for emotional comfort. You may also find it difficult to express your affection for your partner out of fear of being hurt or rejected.

## SECURE ATTACHMENT

Secure attachment is an emotional state characterized by trust, comfort, and safety in relationships. If you have this type of attachment style, you are likely to feel secure and safe when it comes to forming close relationships with others. You may also be able to express yourself freely and trust that your needs will be met without fear of rejection or abandonment.

Secure attachment manifests itself in various ways and is characterized by a few key signs:

- ability to trust and form close relationships
- openness to expressing emotions
- willingness to share feelings and thoughts with others
- feeling comfortable in relationships
- a strong sense of emotional security

The effects that a secure attachment style has on adult relationships can be positive. If you have this type of attachment, you will find it easier to trust and connect with your partner, leading to emotional closeness and joy in the relationship. This can result in healthier communication, a deeper connection, and long-term satisfaction in the relationship.

### Liza's Secure Attachment

Liza, a 28-year-old woman, displays a secure attachment style. This attachment style is formed during childhood when a caregiver provides consistent support and love to the child. Liza had a nurturing and stable upbringing, which allowed her to develop a strong sense of trust and confidence in herself and others.

Liza's parents were always available to her, even when they were tired from work or busy with other obligations. They always made time to listen to her and provide support whenever she needed it. This created a sense of reliability and trust in her relationships, allowing her to confidently form connections with others.

Liza's secure attachment style has had a profound impact on her relationships throughout her life. She can form deep, meaningful connections with others without fear of abandonment or rejection. She trusts her partners, friends and family members, and feels comfortable being honest and open with them.

In a romantic relationship, Liza displays a healthy level of interdependence. She is happy to rely on her partner for support and comfort, but she also thrives when she can provide the same level of care for them. Liza can communicate her needs and boundaries clearly without fear of conflict, but she also approaches disagreements with a sense of empathy and understanding.

Liza's secure attachment style also helps her quickly recover from any relationship-related stress or conflict. When something goes wrong or an argument arises, she can stay grounded and approach the issue with a cool head, which helps her swiftly resolve conflicts.

### Secure Attachment Quiz

Do you think you have a secure attachment style? Here are some quiz and reflection questions to consider:

| | Yes | No |
|---|---|---|
| Do you feel comfortable sharing your emotions with your partner? | | |
| Do you trust your partner completely? | | |
| Do you prefer to resolve conflicts through open communication rather than avoidance or aggression? | | |
| Are you able to maintain a sense of self and independence while in a relationship? | | |
| Do you feel comfortable with physical affection and touch from your partner? | | |
| Do you feel confident in your ability to handle any challenges that may arise in your relationship? | | |
| Do you have a good balance of giving and receiving in your relationship? | | |
| Do you feel comfortable expressing your needs and boundaries to your partner? | | |
| Do you feel secure even when you are physically apart from your partner? | | |
| Are you able to maintain a positive view of yourself, even when faced with rejection or failure in a relationship? | | |

Scoring: Now, add up your "yes" answers. If you answered "yes" to six or more questions, congratulations! You have a secure attachment style. This means you can form healthy, secure relationships with others, maintain your sense of self, and communicate effectively with your partner. If you answered "no" to over five questions, it might be beneficial for you to work on building a more secure attachment style.

Remember, building a secure attachment style takes time and effort but is well worth it for the healthy and fulfilling relationships it brings. Keep practicing open communication, trust, and healthy boundaries, and you'll be on your way to a secure attachment style in no time.

These simple questions and examples will give you an idea of where you stand in your attachment style. Remember, all attachment styles contain a certain criterion; however, this is only to be used as a reference point. Overall, it is important to identify your attachment style so you can take steps to understand yourself and your relationships better. You don't have to live with feelings of worry, self-doubt, fear, and anxiety in your relationships.

## JOURNAL PROMPTS

- Based on the questions above, which attachment style describes you the best? Does one resonate with you more than the other and why?
- Reflect on your past relationships, both romantic and non-romantic. How have you typically approached and maintained these connections?
- Consider the emotions that arise when you think about being close to someone or establishing intimacy in relationships. Do you feel comfortable and secure, or do feelings of anxiety or fear emerge? Explore these emotions and try to understand their origins.
- Imagine your ideal relationship or the type of connection you desire. How does it align with your current attachment style? What changes, if any, would you like to make to create a more secure and fulfilling attachment style?

- Consider seeking feedback from trusted friends or loved ones about your attachment style. How do their perceptions align with your own self-reflection? Are there any insights or observations they can provide that may deepen your understanding?

With proper counseling or therapy, individuals struggling with attachment issues can learn to recognize unhealthy patterns of behavior and build healthy, supportive relationships. And to continue your healing journey, it is now time to acknowledge and accept your attachment style.

# 5

# STEP 5: ACKNOWLEDGING AND ACCEPTING ONESELF

*We can never obtain peace in the outer world until we make peace with ourselves.*

— DALAI LAMA

Self-acknowledgment and acceptance are some of the most important things that you can do for yourself, especially for those with anxiety or PTSD. When you acknowledge and accept your true self, you gain a deeper understanding of who you are, which can lead to a greater sense of inner peace and well-being.

One main reason that self-acknowledgment and acceptance are so important for those with anxiety or PTSD is that these conditions often contribute to a lack of self-esteem and self-confidence. By acknowledging and accepting yourself, you can start to develop a healthy self-image, which can help combat these negative feelings.

In addition, self-acknowledgment and acceptance can also reduce stress and anxiety levels. Often, we are our own worst critics, constantly scrutinizing ourselves and finding fault where there is none. By accepting yourself for who you are, flaws and all, you can start to let go of these negative thoughts and emotions, which can ultimately lead to a more positive and relaxed state of mind.

Another important benefit of self-acknowledgment and acceptance is increased resilience. When you accept yourself for who you are, you become more resilient in the face of challenges and setbacks. You are better able to bounce back from difficult situations, and you have the confidence to take on new challenges and opportunities, even if they seem scary or overwhelming.

Finally, self-acknowledgment and acceptance can also lead to greater levels of personal growth and development. When you practice self-acceptance, you are better able to recognize your strengths and weaknesses, and you can work to build upon them. This can lead to a greater sense of self-awareness, which can help you identify your goals and work toward achieving them.

Now that you know the benefits of accepting yourself, let's dive into what that looks like for each attachment style.

## ACKNOWLEDGMENT AND ACCEPTANCE OF YOUR ATTACHMENT STYLE

Self-acknowledgment and acceptance play a significant role in overcoming insecure attachment styles. Attachment theory suggests that your early life experiences with caregivers shape the way you form relationships throughout your life. Depending on how your caregivers respond to your needs, you develop one of four attachment styles: anxious, avoidant, fearful or disorganized, or secure.

### *Do You Think You Have an Anxious Attachment Style?*

If an anxious person feels like they are asking for too much from their partner, they may avoid expressing their needs altogether. They may also criticize themselves for having these needs and feel ashamed for needing reassurance or support. If this sounds like you, acknowledging and accepting that you are prone to anxious attachment will allow you to reshape the negative views you have of yourself, stop dismissing your needs and emotions, address your insecurities and fear of rejection, recognize triggers that make you anxious, and stop feeling ashamed for needing reassurance and support.

### *Do You Think You Have an Avoidant Attachment Style?*

A person with avoidant attachment issues may feel anxious when their partner expresses too much emotion. They may suppress their own emotions and avoid intimacy in relationships. If this sounds like you, acknowledging and accepting your avoidant style will help you reverse these negative tendencies, begin sharing your feelings without feeling weak or needy, and take steps toward building intimacy to connect with your partner on a deeper level.

### *Do You Think You Have a Fearful or Disorganized Attachment Style?*

A person with fearful or disorganized attachment issues often has a history of childhood trauma or abuse. They are afraid of both intimacy and abandonment, and they cycle between pushing their partner away and becoming clingy. If this sounds like you, acknowledging and accepting your fearful style will allow you to address past trauma, work on self-acceptance, avoid codependent behaviors, and start to accept your partner's love and affection.

And when you have healed enough to enjoy a secure attachment style, make sure to acknowledge that too!

You want to recognize and accept your behaviors so you can create new, healthy, and positive ones that you will repeat. Over time, you will strengthen them and develop new feelings of security. Then you can apply these principles to all your relationships, including with friends, family, and co-workers. And as a parent, being emotionally available and responsive to your child's needs will help them have secure attachments in adulthood.

In the end, always give yourself credit for *any* improvements you have made, no matter how big or small.

## HOW TO BECOME MORE SELF-ACCEPTING

Accepting yourself is a fundamental step toward overcoming anxiety, PTSD, and attachment issues. The process of self-acceptance enables you to acknowledge your positive attributes, embrace your weaknesses, develop a strong sense of self-worth and self-esteem, and ultimately cultivate a healthy, secure attachment style.

Below are a few practical steps to help you on your journey toward self-acceptance:

### *Recognize and Challenge Negative Self-Talk*

Negative self-talk involves an inner dialogue that perpetuates self-doubt, shame, and self-criticism. These negative thoughts and beliefs can significantly impede your ability to accept yourself fully. Identifying negative self-talk requires practice and mindfulness. It involves acknowledging, observing, and challenging negative thoughts or beliefs as they arise.

Once you have identified your negative self-talk, you can challenge it by asking questions like, "Is this belief accurate?" or "What evidence supports this thought?" By challenging these beliefs, you can begin to shift your self-talk toward more positive and affirming messages, which can help you overcome your insecure attachment style.

### Identify Your Strengths

Identifying personal strengths can be challenging, especially if you have experienced trauma or significant stressors. However, recognizing personal strengths is crucial to cultivating self-acceptance. Strengths can take many forms, including empathy, creativity, perseverance, or a range of other qualities.

You can start by creating a list of your strengths, which can help you recognize the value of your unique qualities. Acknowledging personal strengths can improve your self-image and self-worth, promoting a more secure attachment style.

### Focus On Gratitude

Practicing gratitude has been linked to improved mental health outcomes, including increased self-esteem, enhanced social connections, and better overall well-being. Gratitude involves acknowledging the positive things in your life and focusing on positive experiences that have helped you grow and develop as a person.

You can start by creating a gratitude journal, where you write what you are grateful for each day. This can be as simple as the roof over your head or the food on your plate. Practicing gratitude can help you overcome an insecure attachment style by promoting feelings of positivity and self-worth, leading to healthy relational dynamics.

### Embrace Imperfection

No one is perfect, and it's okay to make mistakes. Embracing your imperfections and flaws is an essential aspect of self-acceptance. Individuals who accept their imperfections tend to have more meaningful relationships and a secure attachment style. Embracing imperfection helps reduce anxiety and stress and allows us to live a more fulfilling life.

### Seek Supportive Relationships

Trauma and anxiety can often lead to feelings of isolation and loneliness. Developing supportive relationships can help build a strong sense of community and belonging, which is vital for improving self-acceptance. Supportive relationships can take many forms, including those with friends, family, or mental health professionals.

You can cultivate supportive relationships by participating in group activities, reaching out to others who share common interests, or seeking therapy. Surrounding yourself with secure relationships can promote feelings of safety, comfort, and trust that will enable you to develop healthy relationship dynamics.

JOURNAL PROMPTS

- Do you think you are starting to accept your attachment style?
- If so, write down any negative self-talk or repetitive thoughts related to your attachment style.
- Write down any strengths you think you have because of your attachment style.
- Consider the aspects of yourself that you have struggled to accept. What are the underlying reasons for this resistance? Reflect on the potential benefits and freedom that come from fully accepting and embracing these parts of yourself.
- How do you think you can better practice self-acceptance?
- Reflect on the people in your life who unconditionally accept and appreciate you. How does their acceptance impact your sense of self?
- Explore any challenges or difficulties you may have faced due to your attachment style. How have these experiences helped you grow and develop as an individual? Reflect on the lessons learned and the resilience you have cultivated along the way.

Accepting oneself is a gigantic step toward building your confidence back up and creating secure attachments. Now, you're ready to take the next step toward understanding and improving the wounds that contributed to your insecure attachment style.

# 6

# STEP 6: KNOW YOUR WOUNDS

*Hurt often holds the hidden key to unlocking your greatest healing.*

— BRITTANY BURGUNDER

Your wounds, a.k.a., your trauma, is ultimately what developed your attachment style. From birth to now, you, your mind, and your body have been collecting data and reacting to situations that you subconsciously believe might happen again. By getting to know your wounds, you can begin to heal them and reprogram yourself to think, act, or react differently.

## WHAT IS ATTACHMENT TRAUMA?

Attachment trauma refers to the emotional pain and harm that occur when there is a lack of secure attachment between a child and their caretaker. This type of trauma can have a profound effect on the child's future relationships, including during adulthood.

Attachment trauma can occur in several ways. For instance, a child may have a parent who is emotionally or physically unavailable, inconsistent, or unresponsive to their needs. The child may also have experienced neglect, abuse, or separation from their primary caregiver. These early experiences can cause feelings of insecurity, fear, and a lack of trust in others.

When a child experiences attachment trauma, it can dramatically affect their ability to form relationships later in life. They may struggle with developing deep connections with others, experience intense insecurity, and have difficulty trusting their partners. This can make it harder for them to maintain healthy relationships, both in their personal and professional lives.

It's important to understand that attachment trauma can be experienced in different ways. Some people may experience mild trauma and overcome it through therapy, while others may need intensive therapy to manage the effects of severe trauma.

There are several ways that attachment trauma can be treated. One approach involves working with a therapist to learn how to recognize and understand the effects of the trauma. This can help you develop new ways of relating to others and break negative patterns that may have developed because of the trauma.

Overall, attachment trauma is a serious issue that can have profound effects on relationships and a person's overall well-being. If you or someone you know has experienced attachment trauma, it's important to seek help and support to manage the effects of the trauma and develop healthier relationships in the future.

### What Is Omission Trauma?

Omission trauma is a form of emotional neglect that can occur if your parent or caregiver fails to provide the emotional support, attention, and recognition that you needed as a child to feel valued and loved. This can happen in a variety of different ways, such as when a parent neglects to praise you for your accomplishments or fails to provide emotional comfort when you are upset.

Omission trauma can have lasting effects on adult relationships, as people who experience emotional neglect as children may struggle with attachment and trust issues. If you experience omission trauma, you may struggle to form intimate connections with others and may have difficulty expressing your emotions to your partner. You may also struggle with feelings of low self-worth and self-doubt, as you may have internal-ized the message that you are not deserving of love or attention.

To recover from omission trauma, it is important to seek out therapy and support from loved ones, as well as work on developing healthy coping mechanisms for dealing with trig-gers and anxiety. This may involve learning self-care tech-niques such as mindfulness, developing healthy boundaries with others, and practicing self-compassion.

Ultimately, healing from omission trauma is a process that requires patience, self-love, and a commitment to priori-tizing your emotional well-being. With time, effort, and the right support, it is possible to move past the pain and find a sense of peace and connection in one's relationships with others.

### What Is Commission Trauma?

Commission trauma is a type of psychological trauma that occurs when you experience pain, distress, or negative emotions after being assigned a task, responsibility, or duty that you do not want to perform. This type of trauma can be particularly difficult for people who have anxiety or PTSD, as it can be very triggering and lead to periods of intense emotional distress.

Commission trauma can occur in a variety of situations, such as when you are given a task that you do not feel capable of completing when you are asked to take on additional responsibilities that you are not prepared for, or when you are assigned tasks that conflict with your values or beliefs. This type of trauma can also occur in situations where you have been pressured or coerced into performing a task that you do not want to do.

Commission trauma can have a significant impact on adult relationships, as it can lead to difficulty with trust and intimacy. If you experience commission trauma, then you may have difficulty forming close relationships with others and may feel that you are constantly being asked to perform tasks or responsibilities that you do not want to do. You may also feel that you cannot trust others to understand your needs or boundaries, which can lead to feelings of isolation and loneliness.

To manage commission trauma, it is important for you to learn how to set healthy boundaries and communicate your needs to others. This may involve seeking support from a therapist or counselor who can help them develop coping strategies and strategies for managing their emotions. It may also involve developing a support network of friends and family members who can provide emotional support and help reinforce healthy boundaries.

## EARLY ONSET CAUSES OF ATTACHMENT ISSUES

Some attachment issues can be traced back to specific instances in your life. The following are some common causes of attachment issues.

### Lack of Consistency

Parenting style can have a significant impact on a child's attachment style. Lack of consistency in parenting from early childhood can lead to attachment issues that can last well into adulthood.

If you experience inconsistent parenting, you may struggle to form emotional connections with others and may avoid close relationships. You may feel disconnected and have a hard time trusting others. This can also lead to stress and anxiety in your future relationships, as you may struggle with self-esteem and rely heavily on others for validation.

If you had consistent parenting, you would typically develop a secure attachment style. This means you feel safe and secure in your relationships and can form emotionally healthy connections with others.

### Lack of Support

Parents who are nurturing and supportive create a strong sense of attachment, which helps in building positive self-esteem, confidence, and secure relationships. However, children who lack nurturing and supportive parents might have developed insecure attachments, where they struggle to form and maintain relationships with others. They might not trust others easily and struggle with intimacy in their relationships.

### Lack of Affection

Lack of affection in parenting from early childhood can have profound effects on an individual's emotional and social development. Children who are not shown affection and love by their parents may struggle with attachment issues in adulthood, leading to difficulties in forming and maintaining healthy relationships.

If a child grows up feeling neglected or unloved, they may develop a belief that the world is an unwelcoming and lonely place. Studies have also shown that children who grow up in a non-affectionate environment may be more prone to developing mental health conditions such as anxiety, depression, and post-traumatic stress disorder. This is because the lack of a secure attachment figure can lead to feelings of rejection, worthlessness, and inadequacy.

Furthermore, if you experience a lack of affection during childhood, you may carry these negative beliefs and emotions into your romantic relationships. You may struggle with vulnerability and intimacy, pushing away your partners as a defense mechanism. This negative pattern of behavior can lead to a cycle of failed relationships, reinforcing the belief that you are unlovable and unworthy.

*Absence of Parent or Primary Caregiver*

Since your caregivers have an important role in your attachment style, the absence of a parent can be equally, if not more, harmful to your mental health.

## Divorce

Divorce is a tough time for anyone, but it can be especially difficult for children in their early childhood years. At this stage, children are still developing their sense of security and trust in the world around them. This is why divorce can affect children in such a big way, causing attachment issues or struggles that can persist into adulthood.

When parents' divorce, it can be a major upheaval in a child's life. Suddenly, the family unit they have always known is breaking apart. This can leave them feeling scared, confused, and uncertain about what the future holds. They may struggle to understand why their parents no longer love each other, and they may blame themselves for the divorce.

These feelings can be compounded if the child's parents have a contentious relationship. Arguments, yelling, and general conflict can make the child feel even more unsafe and insecure. They may feel like they are caught in the middle of their parents' problems or that they have to choose sides.

As a result of these experiences, some children may develop attachment issues. They may struggle to trust others or form close relationships. They may become clingy or needy with those they do trust, or they may avoid intimacy altogether. These issues can persist into adulthood and make it difficult for the child to form healthy relationships with others.

It's important to note that not all children will develop attachment issues because of their parents' divorce. Each child is unique and will respond to the situation in their own way. However, as parents, it's important to be aware of the potential impact divorce can have on children and to provide them with love, support, and stability during this difficult time.

## Death

The death of a parent is undoubtedly one of the most devastating events a child can experience in their young lives. For children who lose a parent when they are under the age of 12, the effects can be long-lasting and severe. Studies have shown that children who lose a parent in early childhood are more likely to experience depression and post-traumatic stress disorder than those who lose a parent in adulthood.

The loss of a parent in childhood can lead to attachment issues and struggles in adulthood. Children who experience the death of a parent at a young age may develop insecurities about their safety and security. They may feel abandoned and have difficulty forming meaningful relationships with others. The loss of a parent can also disrupt a child's sense of identity, leaving them feeling lost and unsure of who they are.

The effects of the death of a parent can extend well into adulthood. Adults who experience the loss of a parent in childhood may struggle with trust issues and intimacy. They may also find it difficult to form or maintain close relationships. The trauma of losing a parent can also lead to anxiety, depression, and PTSD.

It's important for children who have experienced the loss of a parent to receive support and therapy to help them process their grief and trauma. Therapy can help children work through their emotions and develop healthy coping mechanisms. It can also help them overcome attachment issues and struggles in adulthood.

## ABUSE AND NEGLECT

Your experiences can shape the way you view and interact with the world. Traumatic experiences as a child and in adulthood, such as physical or emotional abuse, can influence your attachment style and have lasting effects on your mental health and overall well-being. It's important to be aware of the signs of abuse and how they can affect us in order to protect ourselves from further harm and trauma.

Abuse and neglect occur when one partner controls or harms another. This can include physical, emotional, sexual, mental, and financial abuse.

## *Types of Abuse*

There are several types of abuse. Here is a breakdown of the most common kinds of abuse.

### Emotional Abuse

Emotional abuse targets a person's feelings and often manifests through belittling or manipulating a partner, such as using threats to control them. Signs of emotional abuse can include:

- feelings of guilt, worthlessness, and shame
- anxiety and depression
- inability to trust others
- fear of abandonment

Examples of emotional abuse include:

- constant criticism
- name-calling or insults
- isolation from friends and family
- monitoring your social media accounts, emails, or movements
- controlling decision-making

These can all lead to a deep sense of insecurity, making it difficult to form or maintain a healthy relationship.

## Mental Abuse

Mental abuse may include gaslighting or any other form of psychological manipulation that is intended to make a person feel attacked or question their views and way of thinking. This can lead to feelings of confusion, worthlessness, and helplessness. Signs of mental abuse include:

- increased self-doubt
- low self-esteem
- decreased ability to make decisions
- inability to trust others

Examples of mental abuse include:

- lies and deception
- withholding important information
- manipulating the truth
- breaking promises or making false accusations

These can all lead to a deep sense of abandonment and betrayal, leaving the victim feeling completely overwhelmed.

## Physical Abuse

Physical abuse is any intentional use of physical force intended to hurt or harm another person. Physical abuse can lead to feelings of fear, helplessness, and worthlessness. Signs of physical abuse include:

- bruises, cuts, and other visible injuries
- constant fear of their partner
- unexplained changes in behavior
- inability to trust others

Examples of physical abuse can include:

- pushing and shoving
- hitting and slapping
- restraining a partner against their will

**Sexual Abuse**

Sexual abuse can include any unwanted sexual behavior that prevents or stops a partner from engaging in sexual activities without their consent. Signs of sexual abuse include:

- fear and anxiety around their partner
- withdrawing from social activities or friends
- feeling ashamed or embarrassed
- difficulty trusting others

Examples of sexual abuse include:

- forcing a partner to have sex against their will
- pressuring a partner into engaging in sexual activities they are not comfortable with
- using threats or intimidation to make them do something sexually

These experiences can all contribute to a deep sense of abandonment and betrayal, making it hard for the victim to create or maintain strong, healthy relationships.

**Financial Abuse**

Financial abuse occurs when one partner controls the other partner's access to money or resources. Signs of financial abuse include:

- withdrawing large amounts of money without the other partner's knowledge or consent
- using credit cards without permission
- constantly monitoring spending prevents a partner from having access to bank accounts or funds

Examples of financial abuse can include:

- withholding money from a partner to prevent them from being financially independent
- controlling their partner's access to bank accounts or credit cards
- forcing a partner to take on more debt than they are comfortable with

Financial abuse is an insidious form of control that is often hard to recognize and escape. It can have a long-term impact on victims, making it harder for them to achieve financial independence or build wealth. It can also make them vulnerable to further abuse and exploitation by their abuser.

## EFFECTS OF ABUSE AND HOW THEY RELATE TO ATTACHMENT ISSUES

The effects of abuse on a person's attachment style can be profound. According to research, people who have experienced childhood abuse or trauma have a higher risk of attachment-related anxiety and may have difficulty communicating their needs in a relationship. They may also suffer from a lower sense of self-worth, which affects their ability to form trusting relationships with others.

Besides these challenges, if you have experienced abuse, you may struggle to identify when you are in a healthy relationship. You may be more likely to attract or be attracted to abusive partners because it is something that you are familiar with. You may also have a higher risk of developing unhealthy coping mechanisms, such as substance abuse or self-harm.

The following are some effects of abuse:

- PTSD
- anxiety and depression
- low self-esteem and self-confidence
- trust issues
- difficulty forming secure relationships

People who have experienced abuse may find it difficult to trust others and may have difficulty forming healthy relationships in the future because of their experiences. It is important for people who have experienced abuse to seek professional help and support to overcome their traumatic experiences.

## ABANDONMENT

Abandonment is the feeling of being left alone, rejected, or forgotten by someone important in your life. It can come in different forms, such as physical abandonment, emotional abandonment, or even neglect. When someone you care for leaves you, it can lead to a deep sense of loss, sadness, and anxiety. This can be especially distressing if you have experienced trauma before or have a history of an insecure attachment style.

Abandonment differs from absent parenting in that absent parenting is a more passive form of neglect, whereas abandonment is an active form of rejection. It can create feelings of worthlessness, confusion, and insecurity that can have profound effects on an individual's mental health.

Those with insecure attachment styles may be at greater risk of experiencing feelings of abandonment. For example, if a child grew up with a caregiver who was frequently absent or inconsistent, they may develop an anxious-ambivalent attachment style. This can manifest in adulthood as clinginess or fear of separation, leading to a constant need for the presence and reassurance of others in their lives. In contrast, if a child grew up with a caregiver who was emotionally and physically unavailable, they may develop an avoidant attachment style, which can lead to a deep-seated fear of vulnerability and emotional connection.

Abandonment can greatly affect those with insecure attachment styles, often leading to feelings of low self-worth, anger, anxiety, and depression. These individuals may struggle to maintain healthy relationships with others and often struggle with intimacy or trust. People with severe abandonment issues may become clingy or controlling in relationships, while others may completely avoid close relationships to protect themselves.

Abandonment can also lead to a cycle of negative self-talk where feelings of rejection or inadequacy become pervasive and self-defeating. This, in turn, can lead to self-destructive behaviors such as substance abuse or risk-taking. Moreover, abandoned individuals can become too dependent on their support system, constantly seeking reassurance out of fear of being left alone.

## CAUSES FROM PAST RELATIONSHIPS

Your past relationships can also affect your attachment style. If you have a secure relationship, even if you identify with an insecure attachment, you have a better chance of improving yourself and thriving in your relationship. However, negative relationships that tap into your insecure attachment can either exacerbate it or add additional concerns to your attachment style.

### Abusive Partner

Unfortunately, abusive partners can significantly affect a person's sense of attachment. There are various types of abuse in a romantic relationship, including emotional, mental, physical, and sexual.

If you are in a relationship where there is any form of abuse, it is essential to reach out to family, friends, or professionals for help. The signs of abuse can vary depending on the type, but some warning signs include controlling behavior, threatening, belittling, or name-calling, using physical force during conflicts, and making social or sexual demands.

The effects of abuse on a person's attachment style can be long-lasting, but there are various forms of therapy available, such as cognitive-behavioral therapy (CBT) and eye movement desensitization and reprocessing (EMDR), to address and help overcome these issues.

### Narcissistic Partner

Your past relationships deeply impact your present and future relationships. How you were treated by your past partners can affect your attachment styles, which then affect your current and future relationships. Narcissism is a disorder that can be damaging and take away from a healthy relationship.

Narcissistic partners often display controlling behavior and an inflated sense of self-importance. They may make unreasonable demands of their partner, such as expecting them to constantly show admiration for the narcissist's accomplishments or appearance.

They may become jealous or possessive and engage in manipulative tactics to gain control over their partner. The effects of a narcissistic relationship can be severe and long-lasting. The victim of the abuse may have difficulty trusting others, exhibit feelings of shame or guilt, experience low self-esteem, or suffer from depression or anxiety.

Now let's discuss how a narcissistic partner can affect you. Some effects of being in a narcissistic relationship:

- Your self-esteem takes a hit as your partner constantly puts you down and makes you feel like nothing you do is ever good enough.
- You may start to question your own reality as your partner gaslights you and tries to convince you that you're the one who's in the wrong.
- Your boundaries may be constantly violated as your partner thinks it's okay to ignore your needs and do whatever they want.
- You may have difficulty trusting future partners, as you've been conditioned to believe that relationships

are supposed to be one-sided and that you should always put your partner's needs before your own.

Signs you're in a narcissistic relationship:

- Your partner constantly talks about themselves and their achievements while rarely showing interest in your life or feelings.
- Your partner is extremely manipulative and skilled at gaslighting.
- Your partner has extremely high expectations that you can't possibly meet, and if you can't meet them, they get extremely angry.
- Your partner insists on being right all the time and can't handle criticism without getting defensive.

Understanding the profound impact of past wounds and trauma on your attachment style is crucial. It is essential to recognize how these experiences can shape your ability to form healthy relationships and seek support if needed. If you suspect that you are in a narcissistic relationship, reaching out to a professional can provide guidance in rebuilding your self-esteem and establishing healthy boundaries.

JOURNAL PROMPTS:

- Reflect on any significant life events or experiences that may have influenced your attachment style. How have these experiences shaped your view of relationships and your approach to attachment?
- Write about the emotions that arise when you think about the trauma you have experienced. How do these emotions impact your current relationships and attachment dynamics?
- Consider how your trauma may have affected your self-perception and self-worth. Write down any negative beliefs you may hold about yourself as a result of the trauma.

Adults who have experienced abuse or neglect during childhood may exhibit symptoms of PTSD, including flashbacks, nightmares, and heightened vigilance. The lack of parental support can also contribute to low self-esteem, negative self-talk, and self-doubt.

By understanding the connection between past wounds, trauma, and your attachment style, you can begin to address and heal these underlying issues, fostering healthier relationships and promoting your overall well-being. Seek the necessary support and resources to embark on this transformative journey of self-discovery and healing.

Now that you have explored the wounds that have contributed to your insecure attachment style, let's take a look at how your attachment style is affecting your relationships.

# 7

# STEP 7: THE TRUTH—HOW YOUR ATTACHMENT STYLE AFFECTS RELATIONSHIPS

*According to Buddhist psychology, most of our troubles stem from attachment to things that we mistakenly see as permanent.*

— DALAI LAMA

Your attachment style can affect you throughout your life, even into adulthood. It can influence how you interact with people, how successful your relationships are, and even how you view yourself. Your attachment style can help you create healthier relationships and improve communication with the important people in your life, but first, understanding how your attachment style may affect your relationship is key.

## EFFECTS OF AN ANXIOUS ATTACHMENT

Individuals with this anxious attachment style tend to worry excessively about their partner's love and affection, and often engage in clingy, needy behavior to try and secure a stronger connection. If you have this anxious behavior, it can have a variety of negative effects on relationships, including decreased trust, decreased intimacy, and increased conflict.

One way that an anxious attachment style can affect your relationships is by creating a destructive pattern of behavior known as "protest behavior." This behavior is characterized by actions such as constantly checking in on your partner, becoming jealous or possessive, and seeking attention and validation at all times. While these actions may seem like a way to strengthen the relationship, they can actually lead to the opposite result. Protest behavior can make your partner feel suffocated and trapped, leading them to pull away from the relationship in an attempt to regain their independence.

Another way that an anxious attachment style can affect relationships is by causing a constant sense of anxiety and worry. If you have this attachment style, you may spend hours obsessing over minor perceived slights from your partner or anxiously waiting for them to respond to a text or call. This constant state of worry can lead to emotional exhaustion and an inability to fully engage with the relationship. As a result, you may become more and more withdrawn, leaving the other partner feeling unimportant and undervalued.

Lastly, an anxious attachment style can affect relationships by triggering a self-fulfilling prophecy of abandonment. Because anxious people are so focused on their fear of being abandoned, they may unconsciously push their partners away through their clingy and needy behavior. This can create a vicious cycle in which you become increasingly worried and fearful, leading to further protest behavior and conflict.

### Deborah and Devin

Deborah and Devin have been together for six months, and theirs is a story of a relationship that has been defined by an anxious attachment style. For Deborah, the need for constant reassurance from her partner is almost overwhelming. She wants to know where he is all the time, who he is with, and when he will be back. It's not that she doesn't trust him; it's just that she feels that she needs to be in charge of every aspect of their relationship.

Devin, on the other hand, is more laid back. He enjoys spending time with Deborah, but he also has his own interests and hobbies. However, he finds that Deborah's constant need for reassurance is taking its toll on him. He feels suffocated and trapped in the relationship.

As their relationship progresses, the signs of an anxious attachment style become more apparent. Deborah is constantly seeking Devin's approval, trying to win him over with gifts and gestures of affection. She becomes increasingly insecure, worrying that he might leave her for someone else. Devin withdraws, seeking space and distance from the relationship.

The effects of an anxious attachment style can be devastating for a relationship. It can lead to constant arguments and tension, with one partner feeling smothered and the other feeling neglected. In Deborah and Devin's case, it has led to a breakdown in communication, with each partner feeling unable to express their true feelings to the other.

If left unaddressed, an anxious attachment style can damage even the strongest relationships. But by recognizing the signs and working to address them, couples can develop a more secure attachment and build a healthier, more fulfilling relationship. It's important to remember that change takes time and effort, but with dedication and patience, it is possible to overcome an anxious attachment style and develop a stronger, more loving relationship.

## EFFECTS OF AN AVOIDANT ATTACHMENT

With an avoidant attachment style, you can ultimately lean toward a pattern of emotional distance, independence, and detachment from your partners.

One of the ways in which an avoidant attachment style can impact relationships is through emotional distance. If you're avoidantly attached, you tend to keep your emotions in check and avoid intense emotional situations. You may shut down and suppress your feelings, which ultimately leads to a lack of emotional connection with your partners. In a relationship where emotional intimacy plays a significant role, this can create a situation where you might feel neglected, unwanted, and unloved.

Impersonality is another common trait of avoidantly attached individuals. For example, you may keep your partners at arm's length, often resulting in a lack of engagement with the relationship. In some cases, you may even avoid physical affection or touch. This can create feelings of rejection and hurt within the two of you, further contributing to an emotional barrier.

Additionally, if you're avoidantly attached, you may value your independence and autonomy highly. You may notice that you often prioritize your freedom and individuality over the needs and desires of your partner, resulting in a lack of compromise in the relationship. This can lead to a power-dynamic imbalance and ultimately cause the partner to feel undervalued and unimportant in the relationship.

Moreover, since avoidantly attached people tend to be self-reliant, you may struggle to ask for help or support from your partners in times of need. You may not feel comfortable with vulnerability and may require a significant amount of privacy, resulting in your partners feeling distant and excluded.

### Calvin and Vanessa

Calvin and Vanessa had been together for a year, and everything seemed great. They enjoyed each other's company and had a lot of common interests; however, after a while, Calvin started to act distant, and Vanessa felt like something was wrong. They would go out on dates, and he would be there physically, but emotionally, it felt like he wasn't there at all.

One day, Vanessa brought this up to Calvin, and he didn't really have an answer. She began to research attachment issues and realized that his behavior was a clear sign of an avoidant attachment style. Calvin's behavior showed that he had difficulty showing and expressing his emotions, even to those he cares about.

In their relationship, Calvin would avoid any emotional conversations with Vanessa and would often withdraw whenever she tried to communicate her feelings. He would make excuses to avoid spending time together, saying that he needed his alone time, or that he had work to do.

The effects of their avoidant attachment style on their relationship were clear. Vanessa often felt neglected and insecure, wondering if he had lost interest in her or if he didn't care about her. Calvin's emotional unavailability caused a rift in their relationship, and Vanessa found herself walking on eggshells not to upset him.

Calvin's conundrum shows just how crucial early attachment styles can be in a relationship. An avoidant attachment style in a relationship can lead to a lack of emotional intimacy and ultimately result in relationship breakdown. If your partner exhibits signs of an avoidant attachment style, it is essential to communicate with them, understand their needs, and work together to build a healthy and happy relationship.

## EFFECTS OF A FEARFUL OR DISORGANIZED ATTACHMENT

When it comes to attachment styles in relationships, not all styles are created equal. A fearful or disorganized attachment style can have a particularly negative impact on relationships. If you have a fearful or disorganized attachment style, it's crucial to understand how it can impact your partnerships and what you can do to work through these challenges.

People with this attachment style tend to have a deep fear of abandonment and rejection but may also struggle with trust and emotional intimacy. If you have this attachment, you may vacillate between pushing your partner away and clinging to them intensely, resulting in a confusing and tumultuous dynamic.

One way that a fearful or disorganized attachment style can manifest in relationships is through emotional volatility. With this attachment style, you may occasionally find yourself overwhelmed by intense emotions, including anger, fear, or anxiety. You may lash out at your partner or shut down entirely, making it difficult for your partner to understand and connect with you.

Another common manifestation of a fearful or disorganized attachment style is a fear of intimacy. You may struggle to trust your partner or to open up emotionally. You may worry that your partner will leave you or that you will be hurt emotionally, leading you to keep your distance even when you care deeply about your partner.

Ultimately, a fearful or disorganized attachment style can be incredibly difficult to navigate in a relationship. If you suspect that you or your partner has this attachment style, it's important to understand the root causes. Then you can work on developing new patterns of behavior so you can build healthier and more fulfilling relationships in the future.

### Simon and Carmen

Simon and Carmen started off as a happy couple. They both came from different backgrounds and had opposite personalities, which attracted them to each other.

However, as time went by, the relationship hit rough waters. Simon was insecure about the relationship; he would often accuse Carmen of cheating on him, even when there was no evidence. Carmen tried her best to reassure him, but nothing seemed to work.

Simon's attachment style in the relationship was fearful or disorganized, which manifested itself in different ways. He would become clingy and needy when he thought Carmen was drifting away from him. However, when she got too close, he would push her away, causing a constant push-pull dynamic.

In addition, Simon had some unresolved issues from his past, which affected his ability to connect with Carmen on a deeper level. He had to constantly work on his emotional issues, which left Carmen feeling frustrated and unsupported in the relationship.

Carmen, on the other hand, tried her best to understand Simon's attachment style, but it was hard. She found herself walking on eggshells, trying not to trigger his fear of abandonment. This behavior left her feeling drained and emotionally exhausted.

The impact of Simon's fearful or disorganized attachment style on the relationship was severe. The constant drama and emotional rollercoaster affected the trust and intimacy between them. It made it hard for them to feel secure in the relationship, leading to misunderstandings and conflicts.

## EFFECTS OF A SECURE ATTACHMENT

People with a secure attachment style have a positive view of themselves and their partners, and they feel comfortable expressing their emotions and being vulnerable. This style of attachment can have a significant impact on the quality of a relationship.

If you have a secure attachment style, then you have no problem building trusting and lasting relationships. You are comfortable with emotional intimacy and communication, which helps you foster deeper connections with your partners. You can express your needs and feelings without fear of judgment or rejection.

When a couple has a secure attachment style, they are better equipped to handle conflicts and challenges that arise in their relationship. They are also more likely to provide emotional support to their partners during difficult times.

### Nancy and Ronald

Nancy and Ronald have been in a relationship for three years. When they first started dating, Nancy was insecure and did not trust easily. She had been hurt in the past and was afraid of getting hurt again. Ronald, on the other hand, had a secure attachment style. He was confident, trustworthy, and he provided support and comfort to Nancy.

Over time, Nancy's fears and anxieties dissipated as Ronald continued to show her loyalty and affection. This allowed her to become more relaxed and self-assured in the relationship. She learned to communicate openly with Ronald about her feelings and needs, which he responded to with empathy and understanding.

One way that the secure attachment style manifested itself in their relationship was through mutual respect and positive communication. Nancy and Ronald attempted to listen to each other and validate each other's feelings. They also showed affection and appreciation for one another through small gestures like hugs, kisses, and compliments. This created a loving and supportive atmosphere that allowed their relationship to thrive.

Another way that the secure attachment style manifested itself in their relationship was through their sense of comfort and safety with each other. Nancy knew Ronald would always be there for her, and she could rely on him in times of need. Similarly, Ronald trusted Nancy and could be vulnerable around her. This mutual trust and emotional safety deepened their connection and strengthened their bond.

The effects of their secure attachment style were evident in the health and stability of their relationship. They could overcome challenges together and maintain a strong sense of intimacy and closeness. They also had a deep sense of trust and respect for each other, which allowed them to build a foundation of long-term commitment.

A secure attachment style can look like mutual respect, positive communication, emotional safety, and a strong sense of trust and commitment in a relationship. Nancy and Ronald's story serves as an excellent example of how these characteristics can manifest and contribute to a healthy and fulfilling relationship.

JOURNAL PROMPTS

- Reflect on past relationship patterns that you have noticed in your life. How have these patterns aligned with your insecure attachment style? What recurring themes or behaviors have you observed in your relationships that can be attributed to your attachment style?
- Consider a specific relationship that has been impacted by your insecure attachment. How did it influence the dynamics, communication, and overall satisfaction in that relationship? Reflect on both the positive and challenging aspects.
- Reflect on the ways in which your insecure attachment may manifest in different relationship dynamics, such as friendships, romantic partnerships, or family relationships.
- Imagine an ideal relationship scenario where your attachment style is secure and healthy. Write down all the positive changes that a secure attachment style could bring.

Please keep in mind that just because you may identify with a certain insecure attachment, it doesn't mean every relationship or the current relationship you're in will forever be in ruins. Taking the time to really understand your style allows you to start improving it.

As you progress on your journey, you will encounter the unraveling of past traumas and negative relationship experiences, which is a necessary process for developing positive coping mechanisms and cultivating secure relationships.

And now that you have a deeper understanding of how your personal attachment style influences your relationships, the next step is to explore your partner's attachment style so you can both move forward with understanding, empathy, and acceptance.

# 8

# STEP 8: UNDERSTANDING YOUR PARTNER'S ATTACHMENT STYLE

---

*You come to love not by finding the perfect person, but by seeing an imperfect person perfectly.*

— SAM KEEN

---

Now that you understand your attachment style and how it may be affecting your relationship, it's time to consider your partner's. While this might seem like the same information you reviewed in the previous chapters, it's important to remember that a relationship is a two-way street.

This step is important because analyzing your partner's attachment style operates similarly to reverse psychology. To gain insight into your partner's behavior, it is necessary to examine their triggers and negative reactions from your point of view. Doing so gives you insight into how your partner must view you and your actions through their eyes.

While you might think that they act and feel a certain way because of different circumstances, understanding their attachment style can help you better understand them. This is your opportunity to put yourself in your partner's shoes and see if you can view the world from their perspective— then, can you understand why they might do or act the way that they do?

## WHAT IS YOUR PARTNER'S ATTACHMENT STYLE?

Determining your partner's attachment style can be an incredibly helpful tool for improving communication and understanding in your relationship. By understanding your partner's attachment issues, you can learn to provide support that is unique to their needs and create a healthier, more secure relationship.

To determine your partner's attachment style, it is helpful to look for patterns in their behavior, communication, and response to conflict. Here are some key traits and examples to look for in each attachment style.

*Anxious Attachment*

People with an anxious attachment style tend to be insecure and seek constant reassurance from their partners. They may be overly concerned with being rejected, abandoned, or not loved enough. They have a strong desire to be close and connected to their partner, but they also fear rejection and abandonment. Anxious individuals often become dependent on their significant other, leading to a lack of trust and an over-reliance on their partner's affection and attention. Some traits to look for include:

- constantly seeking reassurance
- difficulty trusting their partner
- fearing rejection or abandonment
- feeling insecure when apart from their partner

Example: Your partner may constantly check in with you throughout the day and seek reassurance that you still love them. They may also become upset if you don't respond to their messages quickly enough or if you can't spend as much time together as they want.

In a relationship, an anxious partner may feel jealous and threatened by their partner's interactions with other people. They may experience intense emotions and need constant reassurance from their partner. An anxious attachment style can lead to a draining and exhausting relationship where the partner feels smothered and overwhelmed.

## *Avoidant Attachment*

Partners with an avoidant attachment may be emotionally distant and may have difficulty getting emotionally close to others. They may prioritize independence and self-reliance over an emotional connection. Individuals with an avoidant attachment style tend to feel uncomfortable with intimacy and vulnerability in relationships. They fear being too close or dependent on others, so they often distance themselves emotionally. Avoidant partners may have difficulty opening up and expressing their emotions or may prioritize independence over intimacy. Some characteristics may include:

- difficulty expressing emotions
- preferring to be alone
- avoiding intimacy or vulnerability
- being dismissive of their partner's emotions

Example: Your partner may seem distant or uninterested in talking about emotional topics. They may also be uncomfortable with physical touch or being too close to you, such as sitting too far apart on the couch or not holding hands in public.

In a relationship, an avoidant partner may struggle to connect with their significant other on a deep emotional level. They may avoid discussing important topics or expressing their feelings, which can lead to frustration and misunderstandings. Avoidant attachment style can create distance between partners, causing the relationship to become stagnant and lacking in emotional connection.

### Fearful or Disorganized Attachment

Partners with a fearful or disorganized attachment tend to have conflicting feelings about relationships and may feel uncertain about whether they want to be close to others. They may have experienced trauma or abusive relationships in the past that have made them afraid of intimacy or vulnerability.

Some signs are:

- feeling hot and cold in the relationship
- being easily triggered by certain topics or actions
- feeling uncertain about the future of the relationship
- struggling with trust and feeling safe in the relationship

Example: Your partner may be easily triggered by certain topics, such as past relationships or family history. They may also seem indecisive or unsure about the future of the relationship, even if things seem to be going well.

In a relationship, a partner with a fearful or disorganized attachment style may have a hard time trusting their significant other and may oscillate between seeking closeness and avoiding it. They may have difficulty regulating their emotions and struggle to communicate effectively, leading to misunderstandings and conflicts.

### Secure Attachment

Partners with a secure attachment tend to feel comfortable with emotional intimacy and have a positive outlook on relationships. They can communicate their needs and feelings clearly and trust that their partner will be there for them. They are comfortable with both closeness and independence in relationships. They have a positive view of themselves and their partners and can trust others easily. Secure partners are generally better at communicating their feelings and emotions, creating a deep sense of intimacy and connection. Some examples include:

- feeling comfortable with emotional intimacy
- trusting their partner
- effectively communicating their needs
- having a positive outlook on the relationship

Example: Your partner may be open and honest with you about their thoughts and feelings, and they may feel comfortable sharing intimate details about their life with you. They may also be supportive and understanding when you need it, and they trust that you will be there for them when they need support.

In a relationship, a secure partner creates a stable and supportive environment. They are more likely to have successful relationships as they are capable of meeting their partner's needs while fulfilling their own. Secure partners have a sense of emotional stability, leading to stronger communication and increased levels of understanding.

Understanding your partner's attachment style is crucial for the success of a relationship. Understanding your partner's needs, fears, and insecurities and learning how to meet them will help you form a strong and lasting bond. Being aware of how each attachment style can affect you and the relationship can help you avoid misunderstandings and conflicts, leading to a more fulfilling and satisfying relationship.

It is important to remember that attachment styles are not set in stone and can be changed with intentional efforts, such as through therapy or open communication with your partner. With patience and understanding, you can create a healthier, more secure relationship for both you and your partner.

## WHAT TO DO IF YOUR PARTNER HAS ANXIOUS ATTACHMENT

Understanding if your partner has an anxious attachment style can be crucial for maintaining a healthy relationship. Recognizing these traits in your partner can help you approach the relationship with empathy and understanding, avoiding misunderstandings or conflicts.

Moreover, understanding your partner's anxious attachment style can help you realize that their behavior is not a reflection of your relationship or your love for them. For instance, imagine that your partner becomes distressed when you don't reply to their texts promptly or cancel plans at the last minute. Instead of assuming that they are clingy or demanding, you could recognize that their anxiety results from their attachment style and reassure them that you still care for them and value the relationship.

In addition, having a partner with an anxious attachment can be challenging, but there are strategies that can help you both navigate the relationship in a healthy way. Here are some examples:

- Communicate openly: Let your partner know you understand and accept their attachment style and that you will support them. Encourage them to communicate their needs and emotions, and provide a safe space for them to express themselves without judgment.
- Establish clear boundaries: While it's important to be understanding of your partner's anxieties, it's also important to set boundaries that protect your own well-being. Communicate your boundaries calmly and respectfully, and stick to them consistently. You will read more about setting boundaries in Step 13.
- Be consistent. Anxious individuals often struggle with feelings of uncertainty and fear, and

inconsistent behavior from their partner can intensify these feelings. Consistency, however, helps create a sense of safety, security, and predictability in the relationship and demonstrates that you are reliable, dependable, and committed to the relationship, creating a more stable, supportive environment for both of you.

- Practice active listening: When your partner expresses their fears or concerns, try to listen attentively and empathetically. Paraphrase their words back to them to ensure that you understand their point of view.

- Practice self-care: Taking care of your own emotional and physical needs can help you maintain a healthy perspective on the relationship, and avoid becoming resentful or burned out. This can include activities like exercise, socializing with friends, or pursuing hobbies and interests. We will discuss this more in Steps 11 and 12.

- Provide reassurance and attention: When you make an effort to provide reassurance and attention, you show your anxious partner that you care about their feelings, needs, and desires. This helps create a sense of security within the relationship, which can help alleviate any insecurities or anxieties your partner may have.

- Be Patient: Having anxiety in a relationship can be challenging. When you are patient with your anxious partner, you demonstrate that you understand and empathize with their struggles and that you are committed to supporting them through their challenges. Patience can help create a safe and supportive environment where your partner feels heard, validated, and understood.

## WHAT TO DO IF YOUR PARTNER HAS AVOIDANT ATTACHMENT

Understanding whether your partner has an avoidant attachment style is crucial for maintaining a healthy and successful relationship. This attachment style is characterized by a tendency to avoid close emotional connections and sometimes even physical touch. Partners with this attachment style can exhibit behaviors such as emotional distancing, a reluctance to share personal information, and a reluctance to commit to long-term relationships.

One of the main reasons why it's important to recognize avoidant attachment in your partner is that it can significantly impact your relationship. Partners with this attachment style may struggle in relationships because they may need more space and alone time than other individuals. This can create feelings of rejection or abandonment in their partners.

However, there are a few strategies that can help support a partner with an avoidant attachment style.

- Create an environment of trust and understanding: Allowing your partner space to process their feelings and providing a safe, open environment for them to talk about their emotions can help them feel more secure in the relationship.

- Be mindful of their emotions: Taking the time to really listen to your partner's feelings and pay attention to their emotional reactions can help them feel heard and understood.

- Assume your partner has positive intent: Taking the time to understand why your partner is feeling a certain way can help you come up with solutions together.

- Avoid guilt-tripping your partner: Trying to manipulate your partner into feeling guilty or ashamed for their behavior can be detrimental to the relationship.

- Give your partner space to process: Giving an avoidant partner space when needed is a must because they may need time to mentally prepare and sort out their feelings. On the same note, if you notice your partner has checked out or has gone into "avoidant" mode, save the conversation for later.

- Offer instrumental support over emotional support: Emotional support is important, but it may not be as helpful for a partner with an avoidant attachment style. Instead, offering them tangible support, such as helping out with chores or helping them find a job, can provide them with the reassurance they need.

- Attend outside activities without them: Going to social gatherings or taking part in activities might make your avoidant partner more uncomfortable if they prefer to be alone. Doing activities without them can help give your partner the space they need while still allowing you both to have an active social life.

- Rephrase as a request, not a complaint: Avoidant partners may become overwhelmed by criticism or demands. Instead of making complaints, try to rephrase them as a request that is more specific and tangible. For instance, instead of saying, "You never help around the house," you could say, "Would you mind helping me clean up the kitchen after dinner?"

## WHAT TO DO IF YOUR PARTNER HAS FEARFUL OR DISORGANIZED ATTACHMENT

Partners with a fearful or disorganized attachment style have usually experienced trauma, abuse, or neglect during their childhood, which has created a conflicting and confusing internal working model. They may have experienced inconsistent or erratic behavior from their caregivers, which made it difficult for them to learn how to self-regulate their emotions and develop a consistent sense of self. As a result, their attachment behavior toward their partner can be unpredictable or disorganized.

With this attachment style, it's important to establish a safe and secure environment in which your partner can open up without fear of rejection. To do this, you should be patient, understanding, and non-judgmental when they share their emotions or struggles with you. Try to remain consistent in your behavior, and don't be afraid to set boundaries if necessary. Additionally, provide them with plenty of physical affection, such as hugs and gentle touches.

It is essential to understand a partner's fearful or disorganized attachment style because it will help the non-fearful partner act as a supportive and understanding figure, and prevent unnecessary conflicts that can damage the relationship. The fearful or disorganized partner may experience a high level of emotional turmoil, self-doubt, and anxiety. The non-fearful partner must understand their partner's triggers and needs to offer appropriate support.

Here are some strategies that can help support a partner with a fearful or disorganized attachment style:

- Encourage communication: Fearful or disorganized individuals tend to avoid conflict or confrontation. They may also feel uncomfortable talking about their emotions or needs. Being there to listen and support them without judgment will help them communicate and trust their partner better.

- Learn to be patient and supportive: The non-fearful partner must be patient and offer emotional support as needed. This will help the fearful or disorganized partner feel safe to discuss their emotions and feelings.
- Provide reassurance: Fearful or disorganized individuals lack a sense of security and stability. It's crucial to reassure them of their importance and commitment to the relationship.
- Encourage and support therapy: Fearful or disorganized individuals may require therapy to overcome the effects of trauma and abuse. Encouraging them to seek professional help is an essential step in supporting them.
- Be flexible and understanding: When a person has a fearful or disorganized attachment style, their behavior in relationships can often fluctuate between anxious and avoidant. This can make it challenging for their partner to understand and respond to their needs in a consistent and effective way. So, it is important to understand when your partner is feeling anxious versus when they feel avoidant.
- When your fearful or disorganized partner is feeling anxious: Providing reassurance and support can be helpful. This might involve active listening, validating their feelings, and offering comfort or encouragement.

- When your fearful or disorganized partner is feeling avoidant: Giving them space and respecting their boundaries may be more appropriate. Allow your partner to take time for themselves, and refrain from applying pressure or making demands.

Understanding your partner's style is important if you want to help them feel more secure and understand why they may act the way that they do. However, simply understanding the behaviors isn't enough. To truly begin personal growth, you must start noticing the recurring patterns.

## RELATIONSHIP CHECK-IN

Relationships can be complicated, and it's crucial to check-in regularly to ensure that you and your partner are on the same page. Now that you're aware of your attachment style, your partner's attachment style, and how different types of attachment issues can manifest in a relationship, it's time to create a relationship check-in.

A relationship check-in is a wonderful way to help couples check in with each other and improve their communication. It can also be used as a tool to recognize and address any potential problems or issues that may be occurring within the relationship, while keeping your individual attachment styles in mind.

During this time, both partners can take turns asking questions about their relationship, each other, or any other topic. It's helpful to have a list in advance. When creating your own relationship check-in, it's important to make sure that you include questions that are relevant to both partners. Sometimes, it only takes one good question to initiate a productive dialog. Here are some sample questions you can ask each other to get the conversation started:

- What's really working in our relationship right now? Let's celebrate those things and make sure to maintain them.
- Speaking of celebration, is there anything we're currently celebrating? Let's acknowledge and appreciate those wins together.
- Is there anything that happened in the last week or month that feels unresolved? Let's talk it out and find a solution together.
- Do we feel close and connected to each other? If not, what can we do to improve that connection?
- Do we feel supported by each other? Is there anything we can do to better support each other in our individual goals and endeavors?
- Is there anything we've been avoiding discussing? Let's bring it up and tackle the issue head-on.
- Is there anything we would like to acknowledge or appreciate about each other? Let's take a moment to express gratitude and love.

- Are we fulfilling our responsibilities and commitments in our relationship? How can we hold each other accountable and make sure we're both contributing equally?
- How do we feel about our sexual connection? Is there anything we can do to improve intimacy and passion in our relationship?
- How do we feel personally? Are we living in alignment with the people we want to be? How can we support each other's personal growth and development?
- Are we feeling good about ourselves as a parenting team? Is there anything we can do to improve our communication and partnership in raising our family?
- Are we on track with our big-picture goals and relationship vision? Let's make sure we're working towards our shared future and supporting each other's individual dreams.

Remember, checking in on your relationship isn't something to fear or avoid. Instead, it's an opportunity to deepen your connection and love with your partner, and you'll learn how to further deepen this connection by accommodating both your attachment styles.

# A Moment to Reflect

*"Without reflection, we go blindly on our way, creating more unintended consequences, and failing to achieve anything useful."*

— MARGARET J. WHEATLEY

I'm well aware that there's a lot of information to take in here, and there's a lot to think about as you apply what you're learning to your own experiences. We started our journey with the power of journaling and the importance of mindful breathing techniques in managing attachment anxiety and depression, and it's with this in mind that I want us to take a breather for a moment to reflect on how far we've come and look ahead to the future.

The foundational chapters of this book were designed to equip you with tools to heighten your sense of self-awareness. This is the understanding you need in order to move forward to the next phase of your transformative journey. To find the solutions that will work for your attachment style, you first need an understanding of attachment theory, the characteristics of the four primary attachment styles, and the insights you've been gaining about your own. This will be integral to your success moving forward, and with that in mind, I'd like to take a moment to ask for your help in providing this guidance to more people.

**By leaving a review of this book on Amazon, you'll show new readers where they can find everything they need to not only identify their attachment style, but understand how to work with it moving forward.**

Simply by letting new readers know how this book has helped you and what they'll find inside, you'll show them how important it is to have the full picture if they're to see success on their journey of transformation.

So you've reflected, you've shared... Now it's time to move forward. In the second part of the book, you'll discover the solutions and strategies that are going to enable you to cultivate healthier and more secure relationships. With a solid foundation of self-awareness and understanding under your feet, you're ready to embrace all the possibilities that lie ahead.

Thank you so much for your support. As you move forward on your own journey, those few words on Amazon will help someone else get started on theirs.

**Scan the QR code for a quick review!**

# 9

# STEP 9: START NOTICING PATTERNS AND TRIGGERS

*Until you are willing to learn the lessons, pay attention to details, and become patient with yourself, you will keep repeating the same patterns over and over again.*

— KEMI SOGUNLE

When we talk about patterns of behavior in relationships or attachment styles, we are referring to the recurring ways in which people act toward their partner or in a given situation. In other words, it is the habitual way we tend to behave with others. It is important to note that patterns of behavior can be positive or negative, and can have a significant impact on the quality of our relationships.

For example, let's say that you have a friend who is always late to meet you. Even when you set specific meeting times, they always show up 10–15 minutes late. This is their pattern of behavior. It may seem like a minor issue, but over time, it can have a negative impact on your relationship. You may feel frustrated and undervalued, leading to tension and conflict in the friendship. Alternatively, you may recognize this pattern of behavior and adjust your expectations, avoiding unnecessary conflict.

Patterns of behavior can also be negative and unhealthy, especially in romantic relationships. Sometimes, you may use patterns of behavior to gain power and control over your partner—intentionally or subconsciously. This can include emotional manipulation, isolating the partner from friends and family, and even physical violence. These patterns can be difficult to recognize, especially for those who have experienced trauma or abuse in the past.

That's why it's crucial to be aware of and recognize patterns of behavior in relationships. Identifying these patterns can help you understand yourself and your partner better, and can also help you make more informed decisions about the relationships you choose to pursue. It can also help you identify potential problem areas early on, allowing you to address them before they become serious issues.

## HOW TO RECOGNIZE REPETITIVE PATTERNS IN YOUR BEHAVIOR

Recognizing repetitive patterns in your behavior is crucial for personal development and growth, especially when it comes to changing your attachment style. One way to recognize repetitive patterns is through body awareness. Your body often shows signs of stress or anxiety when you repeat unhealthy behaviors. These signals could be physical symptoms like headaches, muscle tension, or sleep disturbances. So, paying attention to your body's messages can help you identify when you are stuck in a negative pattern.

Additionally, negative self-talk can significantly affect the way you behave toward yourself and others. When you keep repeating negative thoughts, you unconsciously reinforce those beliefs, which can lead to self-destructive behavior patterns. Recognizing this negative self-talk and reframing it in a positive light can help change patterns of damaging behavior.

Evaluating your beliefs is also beneficial for understanding your behavior. Your beliefs shape your thoughts, attitudes, and actions. The way you perceive yourself, others, and the world around you can define your attachment style. Many of your beliefs stem from your childhood experiences, which can impact your behavior and attachment style in adulthood. Recognizing and challenging limiting beliefs is essential when trying to change a repetitive pattern of behavior.

As an example, if you have an anxious attachment style, you may be overly clingy to your partner or fear abandonment. Recognizing this pattern and the underlying belief can help you work toward creating better boundaries and developing trust in your relationship. However, if you have an avoidant attachment, you may not trust easily, and recognizing this pattern can help you work on improving communication and building intimacy.

## SECURE PATTERNS OF BEHAVIOR

In a secure relationship, you can maintain healthy attachments with your partner by effectively communicating your feelings and needs. One of the key coping mechanisms used by those with a secure attachment style is talking to their loved ones about what they're feeling. This not only fosters a deeper connection between partners but also helps both parties feel heard and understood.

Another way to develop a secure attachment style is by writing down your thoughts and feelings. This can be especially helpful during times of high stress or turmoil, as it allows you to process your emotions more clearly and with greater self-awareness.

In addition to these coping mechanisms, those with a secure attachment style may also try meditation or therapy to help facilitate emotional regulation. Mindfulness practices like meditation have been shown to reduce symptoms of anxiety and depression, while therapy can provide a safe space to process emotional experiences and gain insight into one's own patterns of behavior and attachment style.

Exercise is also an important tool, as it can help you relieve stress and increase endorphins. This can be as simple as taking a walk or doing some yoga, or as intense as participating in sports or running.

Ultimately, if you want to promote a more secure attachment style, you have to be more aware of your thoughts and feelings when you're emotional. This allows you to understand your own emotional reactions and better regulate them, so you can communicate effectively and avoid escalating situations. When necessary, you can also remove yourself from an emotional situation if it is becoming uncontrollable, in order to give yourself time and space to process your emotions before returning to the discussion.

By utilizing these coping mechanisms, you can work on maintaining healthy attachments within your relationships and foster deeper connections with those you love.

## ANXIOUS ATTACHMENT TRIGGERS

If you have an anxious attachment style, it means that you often feel uneasy in relationships and worry about your partner leaving you. When you experience emotional triggers, your anxiety can become exacerbated, making it harder to control your feelings and actions. Here's how you might act in a relationship if you have an anxious attachment style and feel emotionally triggered.

### Potential Triggers for Someone With Anxious Attachment

Here are some common examples that might trigger you if you have an anxious attachment:

- You send a text, but your partner doesn't reply right away.
- Your partner shows inconsistent behavior.
- Your partner forgets important events.
- Your partner acts distant and seems distracted.
- Your partner arrives home later than you expected.
- You get a new haircut or wear a new outfit, and your partner doesn't notice.
- You receive criticism from your partner.
- Your partner doesn't update you on their whereabouts.

### Unhealthy Patterns of Behavior for Anxious Attachment

Constantly thinking about your relationship is a common unhealthy behavior for people with an anxious attachment style. When something goes wrong or you encounter a trigger, you may start to ruminate on the state of the relationship, over-analyzing every little detail. This can lead to a lot of stress and anxiety, which can actually push your partner away.

Additionally, you may focus on potential threats to your relationship, whether or not they exist. This may manifest as jealousy or suspicion, even if your partner hasn't given you any reason to mistrust them. These thoughts can be overwhelming and make it difficult to have a healthy, secure relationship.

Another unhealthy behavior is trying to be as emotionally and physically close to your partner as possible. This may involve seeking affection or intimacy constantly, even if your partner is not in the mood. Over time, this can become exhausting for both people in the relationship.

Another common unhealthy behavior is constantly trying to contact your partner, even when they are busy or unavailable. When you feel triggered, you may feel desperate for reassurance and seek constant contact with your partner to help ease your anxiety. But this can be suffocating and may push your partner away.

During arguments or conflicts, you may resort to blaming or guilting the other party to get what you want. This can be a defense mechanism to protect against the fear of rejection or abandonment. However, it can also damage the relationship and erode trust.

Finally, you may become angry, even if this anger is directed at yourself. When triggered, you may feel overwhelmed with negative emotions you don't know how to express or manage, leading to outbursts or lashing out.

## AVOIDANT ATTACHMENT TRIGGERS

As someone with an avoidant attachment style, entering into a relationship can be a challenge for you. With this attachment style, you may have difficulty connecting emotionally in relationships and may avoid intimacy altogether. While your tendencies may differ from others', when emotionally triggered in a relationship, individuals with an avoidant attachment style tend to follow certain patterns of behavior.

### *Potential Triggers for Someone With Avoidant Attachment*

If you have an avoidant attachment, some triggers might include:

- Your partner seems overly eager to get too close.
- Your partner demands a lot of attention.
- Your partner expresses a desire to share their emotions and feelings.
- You experience disapproval when you share your emotions with others.
- You feel a situation is unpredictable or out-of-control.
- You feel like your relationship is taking up too much of your time.
- You feel like a situation limits your freedoms or autonomy.
- You're in a position where you require the help or resources of others to meet your needs.

### *Unhealthy Patterns of Behavior for Avoidant Attachment*

One common behavior exhibited is focusing your attention on things that you can control, such as your career or life goals. For example, if a partner does something to upset you, you may choose to throw yourself into work rather than confronting the issue head-on. This can lead to a sense of distance between partners and ultimately harm the relationship in the long run.

Another coping mechanism is the repression of unpleasant feelings. This may come naturally to some, but for others, it may require conscious effort. Rather than address a specific problem or issue, you may choose to push it to the back of your mind and ignore it until it becomes too much to bear. This can create a vicious cycle of avoidance, ultimately leading to more significant relationship issues.

Also, you may not seek support from your loved ones when you need it. Instead, you may sulk or complain instead of directly asking for support, leading your partner to believe that you are either:

- not interested in sharing your thoughts or feelings with them, or
- you do not trust them with your emotions.

In particularly difficult situations, such as a fight or disagreement with their partner, you may employ pre-emptive strategies such as breaking up with your partner to cope

144 | LEIGH W. HART

with your feelings. By doing so, you revert to old behaviors that make you feel more comfortable and in control. However, this can ultimately harm the relationship's trust and stability and cause more significant problems in the future.

## FEARFUL OR DISORGANIZED ATTACHMENT TRIGGERS

If you have a fearful or disorganized attachment style in a relationship and feel emotionally triggered, your behavior might be unpredictable and confusing for your partner. You may struggle with opening up about your emotions and even report that you don't feel anything at all. This difficulty in expressing your feelings can often result in angry outbursts or withdrawal from your partner.

### *Potential Triggers for Someone With Fearful or Disorganized Attachment*

If you possess a fearful or disorganized attachment style, you may find yourself contending with a mix of anxious and avoidant triggers. Consequently, every bullet point covered in the last two sections holds relevance for individuals with this attachment style. As someone influenced by both anxious and avoidant tendencies, you might find yourself more strongly connected to one set of triggers over the other. However, it's important to recognize the interplay of both aspects and the impact they can have on your relationships and personal well-being.

### Unhealthy Patterns of Behavior for Fearful or Disorganized Attachment

Imagine your partner wants to have a serious conversation about the future of your relationship. You might feel afraid and overwhelmed by the idea of sharing your feelings, as you fear rejection. As a result, you might respond to the situation with anger, lashing out at your partner for even bringing up the topic. Alternatively, you might simply shut down and refuse to engage in the conversation altogether.

You create a push-pull dynamic anytime you feel challenged or afraid. You may find yourself caught in a constant cycle of seeking closeness and intimacy while simultaneously fearing and avoiding it. This can lead to mixed signals, inconsistency, and confusion in your relationships.

When someone with a fearful or disorganized attachment style feels triggered, their emotions may fluctuate between intense highs and lows, often experiencing extreme fear, anxiety, and uncertainty when it comes to emotional intimacy. This rollercoaster ride can make it challenging to maintain stable and balanced connections.

Due to past traumas and unresolved attachment wounds, if you have this style, you may have a deep-seated fear of being abandoned or rejected. If something triggers this fear of abandonment, it can manifest as clinginess, neediness, or an excessive desire for reassurance from your partner.

Unconsciously, when triggered, you may engage in behaviors that undermine the success and stability of your relationships. This self-sabotage can take various forms, such as pushing away current or potential partners, creating conflicts, or engaging in self-destructive behaviors.

The reason for these patterns of behavior lies in your attachment style. A fearful or disorganized attachment style is often rooted in childhood experiences of neglect, abuse, or inconsistent caretaking. These experiences can lead to a sense of mistrust and confusion around relationships, making it difficult for you to feel safe or secure with your partner.

Overcoming these patterns can take time and effort, but it is possible. One of the first steps is to recognize the impact of your attachment style on your current relationship. This can involve talking to a therapist or counselor who can help you identify and work through your emotional triggers.

You may also benefit from practicing self-care techniques such as mindfulness, meditation, or yoga. We will discuss this more in Step 11. Self-care practices can help you become more attuned to your emotional state and develop a greater sense of self-awareness.

## JOURNAL PROMPTS

- If you are single, what is it about dating that triggers you?
- If you are in a relationship, what actions from your partner trigger you?
- Can you pinpoint the moment in time when you start to feel triggered?
- How do you react when triggered?
- How would you like to react?

Ultimately, it's important to remember that it's never too late to change your attachment style and create a healthier, more fulfilling relationship. By acknowledging your insecurities and taking steps to work through them, you can learn to trust yourself and others and feel more secure in your relationships. Now that you have learned about unhealthy responses to triggers for each attachment style, let's move on to Step 10, where you will learn positive ways to address your triggers.

# 10

# STEP 10: LET'S BREAK THE PATTERN AND START THE CHANGE

*Bad beliefs make bad behavior.*

— WARREN AKIN CANDLER

Now that you're more aware of the patterns you might have, you may face a lot of emotions. You may feel guilty about your past actions, ashamed for not recognizing the pattern sooner, and frustrated about where you are now. These feelings are normal and valid. Please take a moment to acknowledge them and accept them.

Now, the good thing is that you can improve your behaviors —no matter how long you've been engaging in them. It's time to break this negative cycle and start making positive changes in your life.

## CHALLENGES OF CHANGING NEGATIVE BEHAVIOR

Changing negative behavior can be a difficult and challenging process. It can be hard to break out of the habits and patterns we have become comfortable with, and it's difficult to find the motivation to make the change. Here are some of the key challenges to changing negative behavior:

- Lack of consequences: It's hard to stay motivated to make a change when there is no immediate or tangible consequence for not doing so. For example, if you are trying to break a bad habit like smoking, you may be less likely to stay motivated if there are no immediate consequences if you don't quit.
- Lack of feedback: Feedback is crucial for changing behavior. Without feedback, it is difficult to make adjustments and monitor progress. For instance, if you are trying to break a bad habit like overeating, you may not be aware of all your snacking habits without feedback from other people or yourself.
- Lack of autonomy: When you feel like you're being controlled or told what to do by external sources, it's difficult to stay motivated to make a change because you lack the autonomy to do so.

- Lack of environment or support: Your environment or the people around you can be a substantial source of support and motivation when trying to make a change. If your environment or social circle is hostile or unsupportive, it can be difficult to stay motivated to make a change.
- Lack of social proof: It's difficult to stay motivated if no one else around you is making the same change. Seeing other people do the same thing and be successful at it can help you get in the right frame of mind to improve.
- Don't use the tools: If you have all the tools and resources available to help make a change but don't use them, it can be difficult to stay motivated and make progress.
- Motivated by negative emotion: Many people are triggered to make a change when they feel negative emotions like guilt or shame. While this can be a source of motivation, it is not a sustainable or healthy way of making a change in the long-term.
- Take on too much too quickly: Trying to make too many changes at once can be overwhelming and lead to burnout. For instance, if you try to change your diet, exercise habits, and sleeping patterns all at once, it might be too much. It's better to focus on one change at a time and build momentum as you go.
- Fallen into the trap of thought distortions and biases: We all have biases and thought distortions that can

lead us to make decisions that are not in our best interests. It is important to be aware of these biases and patterns of thinking that could lead us to make bad decisions.

- No commitment: Making a commitment to yourself and setting goals can help you stay motivated and make progress. If you don't have a goal or plan, it can be difficult to stay motivated and make progress.
- You underestimate how tough change can be: Change is not easy. It can take time, effort, and dedication to make a lasting change in your life. If you underestimate how hard it can be, you may not be prepared for the challenges that come with making a change.

Making a change requires commitment, dedication, and hard work. It is important to be aware of the challenges you may face when making a change and to have the tools and support you need to stay motivated and on track.

## HOW TO COPE WITH YOUR TRIGGERS

Many challenges and triggers might stand in your way, but if you know how to combat them, your confidence will grow over time.

## *What Is Self-Regulation?*

Self-regulation refers to your ability to manage your own emotions, behaviors, and thinking patterns. It is a crucial aspect of your mental and emotional well-being as it plays a crucial role in maintaining healthy relationships with yourself and with others. Self-regulation is also essential to improving your attachment style.

The importance of self-regulation in improving attachment styles cannot be overemphasized. Self-regulation helps you manage your emotions and behaviors in a way that promotes positive interactions with others. For instance, if you can regulate your emotions, you are less likely to react impulsively, which can help build stronger and healthier relationships. Moreover, you are more likely to demonstrate empathy, respect, and consideration toward others, which strengthens your attachments to them.

If you have experienced adverse childhood experiences or trauma, self-regulation may be particularly challenging. You may struggle with regulating your emotions, behaviors, and thoughts, which can lead to difficulties in building positive attachments with others. However, through the adoption of self-regulation techniques such as mindfulness, cognitive-behavioral therapy, and other self-care practices, individuals can learn how to manage their emotions, behaviors, and thoughts, thus improving their ability to form healthy attachments with others.

For example, let's consider a child who has experienced a tough home life and has had limited opportunities to learn self-regulation skills. As this child grows up, he or she may struggle with managing their emotions, leading to outbursts or impulsive behaviors. In turn, this may make it difficult for the child to form positive attachments with others since they may not understand how to interact with others in a healthy way. However, if this child learns self-regulation skills through therapy, for instance, they can learn how to manage their emotions and behaviors, thus improving their ability to build healthy and positive attachments with others.

### Using Self-Regulation to Cope With Emotional Triggers

Trauma and emotional wounds are common experiences that can have a lifelong impact on your mental and emotional health. They might manifest themselves distinctly in different individuals, but the common theme is that they have the power to create a cascading effect and impact multiple areas of one's life. While your attachment style can play a crucial role in how you react to emotional wounds, incorporating self-regulation tools can significantly aid the healing process, regardless of one's attachment style.

- Firstly, using self-regulation tools helps to ground you in the present moment by detaching from the distressing emotions and feelings that contribute to emotional wounds and trauma. Grounding can occur through activities such as meditation, deep breathing, or focusing on the five senses. For example, during meditation, you pay attention to your breath, which helps to calm your mind and body and brings you to the present moment. This way, you become more aware of your feelings and emotions, which assists you in recognizing triggers that cause emotional wounds and trauma.

- Secondly, self-regulation strategies help you center yourself, which is necessary to cope with the emotional experiences that contribute to trauma and wounds. When centered, you gain the strength and stability to deal with challenges without losing your purpose and balance. This way, you can identify your values, core beliefs, and strengths that have been diminished or damaged by emotional wounds and trauma. Centering makes it easy to focus on your needs and helps you trust your intuition to solve problems associated with your emotional wounds and traumas.

- Thirdly, self-regulation strategies allow you to focus on the present rather than reliving the negative events that contribute to trauma and wounds. Focusing on the present helps you avoid distractions, stress, and anxiety that limit your ability to move forward. By incorporating mindfulness techniques into your self-regulation practices, you can direct your mind, focus on the present moment, and observe your emotions and feelings without judgment. This allows you to create new neural pathways that can help you manage your stress response and promotes your ability to heal from emotional wounds and trauma.

- Lastly, self-regulation tools help you relax, which is critical to helping you heal from emotional wounds and trauma. Relaxation activities such as yoga, deep breathing, and meditation promote a sense of calmness and ease, which lowers stress levels and improves your overall wellness. Relaxation also helps boost your immunity, lower your blood pressure, and improve your sleep quality, which are necessary for your recovery journey.

From there, you can raise awareness of your reactions and understand how they feel in your body. You may react impulsively to situations that trigger unresolved emotional wounds. Taking the time to recognize your reactions allows you to pause, reflect, and respond to the situation with intentionality, which drastically reduces the risk of spiraling out-of-control.

Afterwards, you can work on changing your negative beliefs. Your beliefs shape your perception of yourself and the world around you, and a negative belief can lead to patterns of behavior that harm us in the long run. Overcoming these negative beliefs by replacing them with positive ones and acting "as if" empowers you to take back control of your emotions and respond to situations with a more positive mindset.

It's important to seek professional help in situations where self-regulation tools aren't enough. Counseling and therapy can help bring unconscious emotions and triggers to the surface and help individuals unlearn negative patterns of behavior. Grounding oneself by detaching, centering, focusing, breathing, and then relaxing is an excellent way to combine self-regulation tools with professional help in the healing process.

### *Healthy Self-Regulation Ideas for Anxious Attachment*

The fear of abandonment, insecurity, and the belief that you are not enough can cause emotional distress and anxiety. However, it's important to know that anxious attachment is not permanent and that there are ways to heal from it.

One of the most effective ways to heal from anxious attachment is to use self-regulation tools. Self-regulation tools offer you the opportunity to become more self-aware, identify triggers that cause anxiety, and learn how to cope with your emotions.

Here are some self-regulation techniques that can help you heal from anxious attachment:

- Regulating your nervous system: Your nervous system plays a vital role in your response to stress and anxiety. When your nervous system is activated, you tend to feel anxious or overwhelmed. Therefore, it's essential to manage your nervous system's responses by engaging in activities like deep breathing, exercise, or even taking a warm bath.

- Externalize your feelings: Often, people with anxious attachment tend to internalize their feelings, leading to more anxiety and stress. Externalizing your emotions involves expressing your feelings through writing or talking with someone you trust. This activity can help you feel more validated and reduce the anxiety associated with keeping emotions bottled up.

- Reparenting your inner child: Your inner child is the part of you that has experienced trauma and anxiety in the past. Reparenting your inner child involves nurturing and caring for this part of yourself by engaging in activities that make you feel safe, loved, and secure.

- Practicing regular self-care: Self-care is essential for your overall well-being. This can include doing activities that make you feel happy, prioritizing rest and relaxation, or even taking care of your physical health by eating well and getting enough sleep.

- Practice mindfulness communication: Mindfulness communication involves being present in your conversations and actively listening to others. Anxiety can cause individuals to have difficulty communicating effectively, and practicing mindfulness communication can help reduce the anxiety associated with communication.

- Know your worth: It's essential to understand that you are valuable and worthy of love and respect. Individuals with anxious attachment often struggle with believing that they are enough. Recognizing that you are worthy can help increase self-esteem and reduce anxiety.

- Change your thinking patterns: Negative thought patterns can be toxic and cause immense stress and anxiety. Changing your thinking patterns involves challenging your negative thoughts, replacing them with positive ones, and reframing your beliefs about yourself and others.

### Healthy Self-Regulation Ideas for Avoidant Attachment

If you have this attachment, you may often have negative beliefs about yourself and your ability to form lasting, healthy relationships. Therefore, using self-regulation tools can help you build more stable and fulfilling relationships:

- Focus on mutual support: Building secure relationships is often challenging if you have avoidant attachment. Therefore, it's important to focus on mutual support and developing a sense of trust in relationships. This can include taking time to understand the other person's needs and providing them with emotional support when needed.

- Distract yourself from intrusive thoughts: Intrusive thoughts can cause distress and anxiety, so it's important to find activities that help you distract yourself from them. This could include engaging in activities like reading, exercising, or spending time outdoors.
- Find a secure partner: Avoidant attachment often causes difficulties in relationships, so it's important to find a secure partner who can provide you with the support and understanding that you need. This could include someone who is understanding, non-judgmental, and patient.
- Be aware of your negative standpoints: Avoidant individuals often have difficulty recognizing and expressing their feelings, so it's essential to be aware of your negative standpoints. This can help you be more in tune with your emotions and understand how to manage them.
- Create a relationship gratitude list: A relationship gratitude list can help you recognize the positive aspects of your relationships. This could include writing down things that you appreciate about your partner or friends and reflecting on those moments.
- Identify your strategies for avoiding: It's important to be aware of your strategies for avoiding. This could include engaging in activities like procrastination, numbing yourself with substances or activities, or avoiding difficult conversations.

- Forget your exes or "the one that got away": Moving on from past relationships can be difficult, but it's essential to let go of any unhealthy attachments you may have. Focusing on the present and developing new, healthy relationships can help you move on.

### Healthy Self-Regulation Ideas for Fearful or Disorganized Attachment

When we experience a fearful or disorganized attachment, it can be incredibly difficult to manage our emotions and responses. However, using self-regulation tools can make a world of difference when it comes to healing and moving forward.

- Allow time and space to process your emotions: It can be tempting to push your emotions aside or try to distract yourself from them, but this only leads to more difficult emotions down the line. Instead, you need to give yourself permission to feel and process your emotions fully. For example, you might journal about your feelings, attend therapy, or talk to a trusted friend.
- Notice the triggers from within: When you become aware of the physical sensations that arise when you feel triggered, you can catch yourself before you react in a way that may be harmful or counterproductive. For example, if you notice tension in your chest or a racing heart when your

partner does something that triggers you, you can take a moment to breathe deeply and center yourself before responding.

- Pause and recalibrate: When you feel triggered or overwhelmed, it can be difficult to think clearly or make informed decisions. By taking a step back and giving ourselves a moment to breathe, we can regain our sense of clarity and control. Taking the time to pause allows for breathing exercises, mindfulness practices, and positive affirmations.
- Create a self-care routine: Creating a self-care routine can help you manage fear and disorganized attachment. Self-care activities can include journaling, exercising, listening to music, and taking baths.
- Communicate effectively and assertively: When you can express your needs and boundaries in a clear and respectful way, you can avoid getting caught up in patterns of conflict or detachment. This might involve using "I" statements to assert your needs, validating the other person's feelings, and brainstorming solutions together.

## CHANGE YOUR MINDSET

Your mindset is powerful, and if you're using that to think negatively, then you won't experience life to its fullest. If you give into your attachment style, you're likely to repeat your patterns. However, little by little, you can improve your mindset and become a more positive and vibrant you.

### Ways to Change Your Mindset

One way to shift your mindset is to recognize and change your thoughts. Negative thoughts can become ingrained in our minds, and it's difficult to recognize them, but it is important to be aware of them in order to make a change. When you become aware of a negative thought, challenge it. Ask yourself if the thought is helping or hindering your progress. If it is hindering your progress, replace it with a positive thought.

Another way to change your mindset is to practice positive affirmations. Positive affirmations are statements that you repeat to yourself that are positive and empowering. For example, if you want to become more successful at work, you could say, "I am capable of achieving success," or "I have the power to make positive changes in my life."

It is also important to focus on the present moment. When you focus on the present moment, it is easier to recognize and shift your negative thoughts. It is also important to be mindful of your emotions and recognize when you are feeling overwhelmed or stressed. When this happens, take a few moments to practice deep breathing and focus on the present moment.

## CHANGING NEGATIVE BEHAVIORS

Now that you can challenge your thoughts and improve your mindset, it's time to begin working on the negative behaviors you want to rewire.

### *Being Accountable*

One of the most important steps in changing negative behaviors is to be accountable for them. This means being aware of when you are engaging in the behavior and taking responsibility for it. You can do this by reflecting on the situation, acknowledging your role in it, and then taking steps to address the problem.

For example, if you find yourself snapping at your partner or children more often than you would like, take a moment to pause and think about what led to the outburst. Did you feel overwhelmed? Did something else cause the outburst? By recognizing this, you can start to identify potential triggers and take steps to address them.

### *Revisiting the Situation*

Sometimes, negative behaviors stem from a misunderstanding or misinterpretation of an event or situation. Before you make any changes, it is important to revisit the situation and make sure you have a full understanding of what happened. This is especially important if the behavior was directed at someone else, as it can help you prevent a similar issue from happening in the future.

If you find yourself becoming angry with your boss during a meeting, take a step back and ask yourself if you fully understand what was said and how it was said. By understanding the context of the situation, you can take steps to adjust your behavior accordingly.

### Be Gentle Toward Yourself

Changing negative behaviors can be difficult, and it is important to be gentle with yourself throughout the process. Acknowledge that it takes time to make changes and be patient with yourself as you work to cultivate healthier habits. Remind yourself that you are capable of change and that you can create positive, lasting behaviors.

### Determine the Triggers and Patterns—Then Change Them

Once you have identified the negative behaviors you are engaging in, it is important to take a step back and identify the triggers and patterns that lead to them. This can help you better understand the behavior and why it is occurring. Once you have identified the triggers and patterns, you can begin to modify them. For example, if you find yourself getting angry when someone interrupts you, take a step back and identify why you are feeling this way. Is it because you feel your opinion is not valued? By recognizing this, you can work on communicating more effectively and expressing yourself in a healthier way.

## *Keep It Simple*

When it comes to changing negative behaviors, it is important to keep it simple. Start with small changes and gradually move toward larger ones. This will help ensure that you are moving forward in a positive direction without overwhelming yourself or feeling like you are taking on too much at once.

## *Keep Practicing*

Finally, it is important to keep practicing your new behaviors. Change takes time, and it is important to keep working on it even if you do not see immediate results. Remind yourself that you can make positive changes, and that it takes time to create lasting habits.

## JOURNAL PROMPTS

- List the challenges you are facing that are hindering you from changing negative behaviors.
- Based on your attachment style, list a few self-regulation techniques that you think will work for you.
- Reflect on Your Negative Patterns: Take some time to identify and write down the negative patterns of behavior that you would like to break.
- What specific behaviors or reactions do you engage in that contribute to unhealthy dynamics? How do

these patterns manifest in different situations or
with different people?

- Explore Your Triggers: Consider and write down the
triggers that activate negative patterns or behaviors
within you. What situations, words, or actions tend
to provoke an emotional response?
- How can you challenge and reframe negative
thoughts, beliefs, or self-perceptions that contribute
to unhealthy, insecure behaviors?

This information might seem overwhelming, and that's okay.
Although change cannot be done overnight—no matter how
hard you try—small, incremental changes can lead to monu-
mental results in the long term. Now that you have acknowl-
edged negative behaviors you might have and how to use
self-regulation techniques to cope with your triggers, it's
time to learn how to take care of yourself while healing.

# 11

# STEP 11: WORK ON YOURSELF: TAKE CARE OF YOU

*Keep taking time for yourself until you are you again.*

— LALAH DELIA

Self-care refers to the intentional practice of taking care of oneself physically, mentally, and emotionally. It involves setting aside time to engage in activities that promote physical and emotional well-being and reduce stress levels. Self-care can include things like exercising, eating well, getting enough sleep, spending time in nature, practicing meditation, pursuing hobbies, spending time with loved ones, and taking breaks from work.

Self-care is of vital importance when healing from insecure attachment issues. It helps us to manage stress, prevent burnout, and maintain physical and emotional balance. Self-care can reduce the risk of developing anxiety or depression and can help individuals manage existing mental health conditions. Engaging in regular self-care also helps promote self-esteem, confidence, and a positive sense of self-worth.

Here are some examples that illustrate why self-care is important:

- Maya is a full-time student with a part-time job. She spends her days juggling classes, assignments, work, and extracurricular activities. By the time the weekend rolls around, she's usually so exhausted that she just wants to sleep, but she knows that taking time for self-care will help her recharge and feel better in the long run. So, she goes for a walk in the park, catches up with friends, or does some yoga, knowing that it will help her feel more energized and alert for the upcoming week.
- Raj is a busy professional who works long hours and often feels stressed out. He decided to take up running as a form of self-care, and he finds that it helps him cope with the demands of his job. He goes for a run every morning before work, and he has more energy and focus throughout the day. He also enjoys the sense of accomplishment that comes with setting and achieving fitness goals.

- Nikita is an artist who finds that self-care is essential to her creative process. She takes time every day to paint, draw, or write, knowing that it helps her stay grounded and connected to her passions. She also sets aside time to meditate, do some yoga, or take a walk in nature, as she knows these activities will help her feel more relaxed and inspired.

Prioritizing self-care is a highly individualized practice, and it's essential to discover what resonates best with you. Take intentional steps towards nurturing your physical, mental, and emotional well-being, embracing the practices that bring you the most benefit. While this chapter will be short, concise, and to the point, its message is profound: self-care is absolutely vital. It may seem like a simple concept, but its impact on your healing journey and the cultivation of secure connections cannot be overstated. To truly heal and thrive, caring for yourself is non-negotiable. Dedicate time to engage in activities you love, which bring relaxation and immense joy. Remember, making self-care a priority is of utmost importance.

## HOW TO BUILD A SELF-CARE ROUTINE

Integrating self-care into our daily lives is crucial for overall well-being. If you're seeking to establish your personalized self-care routine, you're in the right space. Discovering a routine that suits your needs is within reach, and here are a few straightforward steps to guide you along the way.

### Reflect on What Makes You Feel Centered, Calm, and Grounded

The first step in creating a self-care routine is to think about the activities that make you feel centered, calm, and grounded. For example, you may find that taking a walk in nature, practicing yoga, or reading a book helps you feel more relaxed and centered.

### Brainstorm Ways to Incorporate These Activities Into Your Daily Routine

Once you have identified the activities that make you feel centered, calm, and grounded, it's time to brainstorm ways to incorporate them into your daily routine. If you enjoy taking walks in nature, try to schedule a short walk every day during your lunch break or after work. If you enjoy practicing yoga, set aside some time in the morning or evening to practice at home.

### Set Meaningful Goals for Your Self-Care Routine

To make your self-care routine more effective, it's important to set some goals that are meaningful to you. For example, you might set a goal to practice yoga for 20 minutes every day for a month or to take a 30-minute walk every weekday for three weeks.

*Make Changes and Adjustments Along the Way*

Creating a self-care routine is a process, and it's important to be flexible and make changes along the way. If you find certain activities aren't working for you, try something else. If you're feeling overwhelmed with your routine, scale it back.

*Seek Help or Support When Needed*

Don't be afraid to seek help or support when creating your self-care routine. This could come from a therapist, a support group, or a friend who can help keep you accountable.

Overall, it's important to remember that creating a self-care routine doesn't have to be perfect. It's about finding what works for you and making small steps toward feeling centered, calm, and grounded. Remember to take it one day at a time and enjoy the process.

JOURNAL PROMPTS

- List small changes you would like to make to improve your daily routine.
- List 2–3 self-care ideas you like and set an expectation for how often:
- Example: I would like to start taking walks three times a week. Or I want to start meditating every

morning. I want to prioritize pedicures or seeing the chiropractor monthly, etc.

In closing, remember that self-care is an essential component in healing attachment issues. By nurturing your physical well-being, you lay the groundwork for personal growth. As we transition to the next chapter, you will explore the importance of working on your mental strength, while discovering strategies to cultivate a positive mindset.

# 12

# STEP 12: WORK ON YOURSELF—MENTAL STRENGTHENING

---

*As soon as you trust yourself, you will know how to live.*

— JOHANN WOLFGANG VON GOETHE

---

Have you ever heard the saying, "Mind over matter?" It's a reminder that no matter what obstacles we face in life, we can overcome them with diligent mental strength. Building mental strength means developing a resilient, adaptable, and focused mindset that enables you to tackle complex situations with ease. Mental toughness is vital for our personal and professional growth, equipping us with the ability to navigate the complexities of our attachment style, overcome challenges, and cultivate fulfilling connections.

Life is full of unpredictable events, and having the ability to stay calm and composed during difficult times can make all the difference. Mental toughness helps you bounce back from setbacks more quickly and adapt to changes more easily. By cultivating a resilient mindset, you empower yourself to take control of your life and work towards nurturing healthy and secure attachments with unwavering determination and fortitude.

## HOW TO BUILD YOUR MENTAL STRENGTH

Mental strength is an important aspect of overcoming attachment trauma. It allows us to handle stress, overcome adversity, and achieve our goals. Building mental strength requires effort and dedication, but the benefits are worth it. In this section, we will explore four key components of mental strength and provide you with strategies to develop them.

### The Four Cs

The four components of mental strength are confidence, challenge, control, and commitment. These factors are crucial for maintaining strong mental health and developing resilience because they help you develop a positive outlook, persist in the face of difficulty, and make healthy choices.

## Control

The ability to control your thoughts, emotions, and behaviors is a critical component of mental strength. When you choose to take control of your life, you are better equipped to handle challenges and make positive changes.

To build mental strength for control, try the following:

- Identify areas of your life where you feel powerless and make a plan to take control.
- Practice mindfulness or meditation to increase your awareness of your thoughts and emotions.
- Set boundaries with people who try to control you, and learn to say no when necessary.

For example, suppose you feel overwhelmed because you have too much on your plate at work. In that case, you may decide to take control by prioritizing your tasks, delegating where possible, and speaking with your manager about your workload.

## Commitment

A commitment to our goals and values helps us stay focused and motivated. When you have a sense of purpose, you are more likely to work hard and overcome obstacles.

To build mental strength for commitment, try the following:

- Set clear and specific goals for yourself.
- Create a plan of action to achieve your goals.
- Visualize your success and stay motivated by reminding yourself of your purpose.

For example, if your goal is to improve your physical fitness, you may commit to a weekly workout plan and track your progress. You may also remind yourself of the benefits of exercise, such as increased energy and improved mood.

**Challenge**

Challenging ourselves is essential for personal growth and development. When we step outside our comfort zone and take on new challenges, we develop resilience and become more confident in our abilities.

To build mental strength for challenges, try the following:

- Identify areas of your life where you would like to grow or improve.
- Break your large goals into smaller, manageable steps.
- Embrace your mistakes or failures as a learning opportunity.

For example, if you are shy and struggle to speak up in group settings, you may challenge yourself to participate in more group discussions and practice public speaking. With time and effort, you will gain confidence and become more comfortable in these situations.

## Confidence

Confidence is a crucial component of mental strength. When you believe in yourself and your abilities, you are more likely to take risks and pursue your goals.

To build mental strength and confidence, try the following:

- Practice positive self-talk and challenge negative beliefs.
- Celebrate your successes, no matter how small.
- Surround yourself with supportive people who believe in you.

For example, if you struggle with self-doubt, you may start by practicing positive affirmations such as "I am capable and resilient." You may also look for mentors or friends who encourage you and believe in your abilities.

Building mental strength is something that we all should strive for. However, it's important to note that it's not an overnight process. Following are a few more tips to help you build mental strength.

### *Focus On One Thing at a Time*

In today's fast-paced world, it's easy to feel overwhelmed by the number of things on our to-do list. However, multitasking can actually hurt our productivity and mental strength. Instead, try focusing on one thing at a time.

For instance, if you're working on a project or studying, set aside a specific time to focus solely on that task. During that time, eliminate any distractions, such as your phone or email notifications. By focusing on one task at a time, you'll be able to complete it more efficiently and effectively.

### Dedicate Time to Self-Care

Self-care is not selfish; it's essential to our mental health and well-being. Taking care of ourselves emotionally, physically, and mentally are great ways to build mental strength.

If you're feeling stressed or overwhelmed, take a break to do something that brings you joy, such as reading a book, taking a bath, or spending time with a loved one. When we take care of ourselves, we have more energy and resilience to handle the challenges that come our way.

### Move Your Body

Our mind and body are interconnected, so taking care of our body is one way to help build mental strength. Moving your body regularly, whether it's through exercise, yoga, or any other physical activity, can help reduce stress, increase energy levels, and improve overall well-being.

For example, if you're feeling low or anxious, go for a walk outside or dance to your favorite song. As you move your body, focus on the sensations you feel—your breath, your muscles, and your surroundings. This will help you stay present in the moment and reduce any negative thoughts.

### Practice a Mindfulness Break Every Day

Mindfulness is the practice of being present, aware, and non-judgmental in the moment. Practicing mindfulness regularly can help reduce stress, anxiety, and improve overall well-being.

You can take a mindfulness break every day by setting aside a few minutes to be present. Sit in a quiet space, close your eyes, and focus on your breath. When your mind wanders, gently bring it back to your breath. This practice can help build mental resilience and promote a sense of calm.

### Set Limits and Boundaries, and Stick to Them

Setting limits and boundaries is an essential part of building mental strength. It's important to know our limits and prioritize our time and energy accordingly.

For example, set limits on social media or work-related emails after a certain time, or say no to commitments that don't align with your values or priorities. By setting limits and sticking to them, we can avoid burnout and cultivate mental strength.

## POSITIVE AFFIRMATIONS TO USE DAILY

Affirmations are powerful statements that can help individuals overcome various life challenges, including attachment styles. Attachment style refers to the way individuals relate to others based on their attachment history. For instance, some people may be securely attached, while others may be avoidantly or anxiously attached.

In healing from attachment styles, affirmations can be useful for boosting self-esteem, improving confidence, and promoting positive self-talk. In this section, we will discuss the importance of affirmations and how they can help you heal from your insecure attachment style.

Affirmations encourage positive thinking, which can improve your mental health. Excessive negative beliefs about yourself can lead to feelings of anxiety, depression, and low self-esteem. Affirmations help to counteract these negative beliefs by bringing positive, uplifting beliefs to the forefront of the mind. For example, instead of thinking, "I'm not good enough for love," an affirmation like "I'm worthy of love and connection" can create a shift in perspective, which promotes mental health and healing.

These positive phrases can help change the way you see yourself and your attachment style. Affirmations can help you reframe your beliefs about yourself, allowing you to see yourself as deserving of love and connection. This new mindset can ultimately lead to more fulfilling and secure relationships with others.

Finally, affirmations help to create a positive self-image. By regularly using affirmations that promote self-love and self-acceptance, you can develop a healthy relationship with yourself. A positive self-image can lead to increased self-confidence, which is essential for creating healthy attachments with others.

Here are some affirmations that can support healing from attachment trauma:

- I am worthy of love and connection.
- I trust myself to form healthy relationships.
- I am deserving of respect and kindness.
- I am capable of creating and maintaining healthy attachments.
- I am enough just as I am.
- I am worthy of forgiveness and peace.
- I will prioritize my emotional needs and well-being.
- I am capable of healing my attachment wounds.
- I will let go of the past and embrace a healthy future.
- My imperfections make me unique and authentic.
- I embrace vulnerability and authenticity in relationships.
- My self-worth is not dictated by the opinions of others.
- I embrace my emotions and allow myself to feel.

- I have the power to change my attachment style.
- I am open to receiving love and connection.
- I am confident in my ability to form healthy attachments.
- I am grounded and centered, no matter my attachment style.
- I let go of fear and embrace love.
- I am in control of my thoughts and beliefs.
- I am grateful for the healing that is taking place within me.

## JOURNAL PROMPTS

- Reflect on your strengths: What are some natural abilities or characteristics that have helped you overcome challenges in the past?
- Challenge limiting beliefs: What are some negative thoughts or beliefs that arise when faced with difficulties? How can you reframe these limiting beliefs into empowering statements that foster positive self-esteem?
- Revisit and use your journaling notes as a valuable resource in selecting or crafting personalized mantras that resonate with you on your journey. Make a list of your favorite mantras and affirmations.

- Choose a quiet place or look in the mirror, pick three positive affirmations, and repeat them enough times until you start feeling better about yourself.
- For example, you can sit quietly, with your eyes closed, and repeat, "I am a beautiful and deserving soul," while envisioning your future, strong, confident self.

Now that you have a few more tools in your box to help you improve your emotions and mental strength, it's time to work on setting boundaries so you can maintain the type of support that you need.

# 13

# STEP 13: SETTING BOUNDARIES

*"No" is a complete sentence.*

— ANNE LAMONT

Setting healthy boundaries is critical to living a balanced and fulfilled life, especially when it comes to your relationships. Boundaries are the limits we set for ourselves and others, defining what is and isn't acceptable in our personal space and interactions. They create a sense of safety, respect, and mutual understanding, and they help establish healthy attachments with partners, friends, and family members.

188 | LEIGH W. HART

## TYPES OF BOUNDARIES

Setting healthy boundaries is an essential aspect of maintaining healthy attachments, whether with friends, family, or romantic partners. It involves knowing what your limits are, communicating them effectively, and respecting the boundaries of others. Failure to set boundaries can lead to resentment, misunderstandings, and even the end of relationships. In this section, we will explore the seven types of boundaries and why it is crucial to set them.

### *Physical Boundaries*

Physical boundaries refer to the amount of physical contact you are comfortable with. You may determine your level of comfort with physical touch, and others must respect and honor that boundary. For instance, a person may not want anyone to touch or hug them without their consent, and it's essential to respect their decision.

### *Emotional Boundaries*

Emotional boundaries involve the ability to identify and express emotions. It is essential to understand and respect each other's feelings without letting them consume you. You must also recognize when other individuals are crossing the line into your emotional space.

### Sexual Boundaries

Sexual boundaries apply to any act of sexual contact. Everyone has the right to their own body, and nobody should be expected to engage in sexual activities that they are not comfortable with. This is particularly true when it comes to consent, which is a fundamental aspect of any sexual encounter.

### Material Boundaries

Material boundaries refer to both personal and shared property. These boundaries help to prevent disputes and misunderstandings when it comes to your finances or possessions and can prevent a lot of unnecessary arguments.

### Time Boundaries

Time boundaries help establish how much time you are willing to spend with others. This is important when it comes to work-life balance and personal time. You should not feel guilty for communicating when you need time alone or time to work on personal projects.

### Intellectual Boundaries

Intellectual boundaries help you establish your opinions, ideas, and beliefs. It is crucial to recognize that everyone has their own unique perspectives and to respect them, even if they differ from our own. Disrespecting others' beliefs can lead to conflict and misunderstandings.

## *Spiritual Boundaries*

Spiritual boundaries are related to your religious or spiritual beliefs or values. These boundaries involve acknowledging and respecting the religious and spiritual beliefs of others. It's important to avoid any behavior that may offend someone or belittle their beliefs.

## BENEFITS OF SETTING BOUNDARIES

Healthy boundaries can foster trust, respect, and communication in any relationship. Communicating boundaries clearly and effectively helps establish a healthy dynamic that is built on mutual understanding and respect for each other's needs. By having healthy boundaries in place, you can protect your emotional and physical well-being, ensuring that you do not compromise your values, priorities, and beliefs.

Having healthy boundaries often leads to better mental and emotional health. When you set and maintain healthy boundaries, you are better equipped to prioritize your needs and avoid feelings of stress, anxiety, and burnout. You can navigate situations more confidently and assertively without feeling guilty for putting yourself first.

This happens because setting boundaries helps separate your thoughts, feelings, and needs from those of others. You can develop a better understanding of what you want, how you feel, and what you need when you take the time to create and communicate your boundaries. You're more likely to achieve satisfaction, happiness, and success in your personal and professional lives when you establish healthy boundaries.

Another benefit of setting boundaries is that it helps you develop independence. When you set healthy boundaries, you're making a conscious decision about what you're willing to accept in your life to create space for what you value. This can help you overcome feelings of obligation and dependence on others, allowing you to assert your independence and take control of your life.

It's also important to recognize that setting boundaries can help you identify potential red flags in relationships sooner. If someone is not respecting your boundaries, it is a sign that the relationship may not be healthy. For example, a partner who constantly ignores your need for alone time and emotional space may not have your best interests at heart.

From there, boundaries can also help prevent future conflicts. When you communicate your boundaries early in a relationship, you create a clear understanding of your expectations and limits, which can prevent misunderstandings, disagreements, and arguments later on. For example, if you're in a romantic relationship and your partner knows your boundaries around communication, respect, and showing affection, it's more likely your relationship will be harmonious and happy. This can prevent the unnecessary buildup of resentment, which can lead to more significant issues down the line.

This can also prompt stronger or more enriching relation-ships. When you communicate your boundaries with friends and family, you create healthier relationships based on open-ness, honesty, and mutual respect. You can have satisfying relationships with partners, friends, or family members when you have clear and open communication that respects your boundaries.

And last but not least, healthy and proper boundaries can help you not feel guilty or responsible for the happiness of others. This can be particularly important in toxic relation-ships, where you may feel you have to give up your time or energy for the sake of another's happiness. Setting clear boundaries can alleviate this feeling of responsibility and guilt, which can help you maintain healthier relationships.

Overall, making your needs as important as those of others is another essential benefit of setting boundaries. When you take the time to establish clear boundaries around your needs, you're sending a powerful message that you matter and deserve to be valued and respected. This fosters an envi-ronment of mutual respect and helps you create a stronger sense of identity and self-esteem.

## HOW TO SET HEALTHY BOUNDARIES

Setting boundaries in a relationship can often seem difficult and confusing, especially when trying to balance them with your personal attachment style. However, with some helpful strategies and relatable examples, you can create healthy boundaries within your relationship that support and reflect your attachment style. Here are some tips to get started:

Start early: By communicating your needs and expectations early on, you can prevent misunderstandings and build trust.

- For example, if you have an anxious attachment style, you may need more reassurance and want to establish specific communication routines to help ease your anxiety. On the other hand, if you have an avoidant attachment style, you may need more space and independence, so you will need to establish boundaries around your personal time and activities to prevent feeling suffocated.

Be consistent: Consistency is key when it comes to setting boundaries in a relationship. If you allow your partner to cross your boundaries once, they may continue to do so in the future. Establishing boundaries and consistently enforcing them will help build a strong and healthy relationship.

- If you have established the boundary of no phones during dinner time, be consistent about enforcing this boundary. This consistency communicates to your partner that you value communication and time together.

Refrain from attacking: It's essential to communicate your needs without attacking your partner. When emotions are high, it's easy to blame and criticize, but this can damage the relationship and create further conflict.

- Instead of saying, "You always make me feel neglected," try saying, "I feel neglected when we don't spend quality time together."

Know that asking for space and time is okay: Sometimes, we may need space and time to process our emotions or recharge. It's essential to communicate this need without making your partner feel rejected or abandoned.

- If you have had a stressful day at work and need some alone time, communicate this to your partner by saying, "I need some alone time to unwind and relax. I love spending time with you, but I need to recharge my batteries."

Be honest: Honesty is vital in all relationships. Being truthful about your feelings and needs can prevent resentment and misunderstandings from building up.

- For instance, if you feel uncomfortable with a certain behavior or boundary, communicate this to your partner. Saying, "I feel uncomfortable when you flirt with other people," is much better than internalizing

your feelings and allowing jealousy and resentment
to build up.

Listen to your partner's needs: Communication is a two-way
street. It's important to listen to your partner's needs and
establish boundaries that work for both of you.

- If your partner expresses a need for more quality
  time together, work together to establish a routine
  that works for both of you.

Be respectful: Finally, it's essential to be respectful to your
partner when setting boundaries. Remember, the goal is to
create a healthy and secure relationship, not to control or
manipulate your partner.

- For example, saying, "I appreciate spending time
  with you, but I need some space to take care of
  myself," is a respectful way to communicate your
  needs.

## HOW TO SAY "NO"

We all understand the importance of relationships in our
lives. They are an essential part of our social existence, and
they can provide us with invaluable support, love, and happiness. However, as much as relationships are essential, they
can also be challenging to maintain at times, and saying "no"

can help you maintain boundaries, which is critical for your health.

Saying no can be challenging, especially when it comes to relationships. It can make you feel guilty or even selfish, and you may worry that your "no" will hurt the other person's feelings. However, saying no is fundamental to maintaining balance and setting boundaries in your relationships. It enables you to communicate your limits and expectations clearly, and it shows that you respect and value your own needs and desires.

For example, let's say a friend asks you to attend a party with them. You know you do not feel comfortable in large crowds, and you would prefer to spend the evening at home. In this situation, it is essential to say no to your friend. You are clear about your needs and boundaries, and your friend also has the opportunity to respect your decision and your needs.

But how do you say no without feeling guilty? Here are some tips:

- Express gratitude for the opportunity or request. For example, thank the person for thinking of you or offering you the project.
- Be crystal clear in your response. State your limits and explain why you can't accommodate the request. For instance, say, "Thank you for the invite, but I can't make it because I have prior commitments," or

"I'm sorry, but I'm not interested in taking on any new projects at the moment."

- Offer an alternative if possible. For example, if someone asks you to attend an event that you can't attend, you can offer to connect with them at a later date.

- Give an explanation if you want. This helps to provide context and can help the other person understand better. However, avoid being defensive or overly apologetic.

- Be assertive, polite, and courageous. Learn to stand up for yourself respectfully and express your opinion clearly. You do not need to justify or apologize for your decision to say no.

- Be firm. Do not leave any room for negotiation if you feel uncomfortable with the request. Stick to your boundaries and communicate them firmly and confidently.

- Flip the question back and ask them if they can accommodate you if you're overwhelmed. Instead of saying no directly, reframe the response by expressing your needs and asking if your partner or friend can accommodate them.

- Be selfish. Saying no can sometimes feel selfish, but it is crucial to prioritize your well-being and needs. If you feel guilty, remember that saying no is beneficial for both you and your relationships in the long-run.

- Just say it. There is no need to beat around the bush or sugarcoat anything. Just say no clearly and politely.

In closing, saying no in relationships can be difficult, but it is essential for maintaining boundaries and balances in relationships. Remember to be assertive, polite, and firm when saying no to communicate your needs respectfully. Be selfish, prioritize your well-being, and do not hesitate to say no when you need to. By doing so, you are taking control of your life and building secure relationships based on mutual respect and understanding.

## JOURNAL PROMPTS

- Make a list of boundaries you want to set for your current or future partner.
- Take a moment to reflect and be honest with yourself. Are there any of your partner's boundaries that you have been disregarding? If so, write them down and create a list of actions you can try to adjust your behaviors.
- As you begin to learn more about yourself, as well as your likes, dislikes, and preferences, you can keep adding to this list. This list will come in handy later when it comes time to talk to your partner. When you have that conversation to share your boundaries,

you can also acknowledge any boundaries you may have crossed and strive for improvement together.

Boundaries are crucial to maintaining your autonomy and making sure that you live according to your values—not others'. Now that you're aware of how to create and maintain boundaries, it's time to talk about how you can create healthy expectations for yourself and your relationships.

# 14

## STEP 14: SETTING EXPECTATIONS

*Set the standard! Stop expecting others to show you love, acceptance, commitment, and respect when you don't even show that to yourself.*

— STEVE MARABOLI

Expectations are an integral part of any relationship, be it romantic, professional, or platonic. They are the set of beliefs that you hold about how someone should behave, act, or treat you. When entering a relationship, you have certain expectations based on your personal values, past experiences, and cultural beliefs.

The importance of expectations lies in the fact that they set the standard for how you want to be treated in a relationship. Expectations help you understand your needs and communicate them in a way that makes it easier for your partner to fulfill them. They also help you define your boundaries, which are important for building trust and respect.

Setting expectations might seem like a surefire way to be disappointed, or you might feel as though that is too much pressure to place on yourself or others. However, much like setting boundaries, setting expectations can be an important aspect of any secure relationship. Whether it's with your partner, friends, or family, having clear expectations will not only help you build stronger relationships but also ensure that everyone is on the same page. Plus, setting expectations for how you want your relationship to look and feel can actually help maintain its health and longevity. So, let's dive into how to set expectations in your relationships.

## IS IT OKAY TO HAVE EXPECTATIONS?

Most of us believe we shouldn't have any expectations— that's the simplest and easiest way to ensure that we're not hurt or let down.

Unfortunately, though, we still have expectations, only now they are negative. For instance, you might feel as though it's inappropriate to ask, demand, or expect that your partner will clean the pile of dishes in the sink. So instead of expecting them to do it, you expect the opposite. You expect that they won't do it and that it will be left there for you.

These negative expectations create a negative self-fulfilling prophecy that causes resentment to build. Instead of communicating with your partner about how you expect the dishes or any other issue to be handled, you stew in your resentment and wait for them to read your mind. You see, you might think you don't have expectations, but assuming the worst from your partner is an expectation.

It's okay to have expectations as long as they are healthy. You shouldn't expect your partner to neglect you or their duties, but you should expect your partner to act in a respectful, courteous, and compassionate manner. Listening to and respecting each other is also an acceptable expectation. You should expect to spend quality time together and have your needs met. Also, you can hope that disagreements and conflicts will be handled in a calm, reasonable manner. These expectations are not unreasonable or unattainable. In fact, the strength of solid relationships comes from these very same healthy principles.

Expectations are simply a way to hold yourself and your partner accountable for the relationship that you have created.

When you have healthy expectations for your relationships, it helps both people create an environment of mutual respect, understanding, and trust. Setting healthy expectations can help all parties involved feel safe, secure, and fulfilled in the relationship. It also helps to establish a higher level of communication so that any difficult conversations can be handled in a respectful and productive way. When expectations are unclear, it can create confusion and tension in the relationship. Healthy expectations can help prevent these issues from arising and ensure that both partners feel heard and respected.

For example, you expect your partner to take you out on a fancy date every weekend. However, your partner cannot meet that expectation due to financial constraints or personal preference. This can lead to disappointment and conflict in the relationship.

Effective communication is essential to ensuring that expectations are met. It's important to be clear and specific about what you want and need from your partner and how you expect them to behave. You should also be willing to listen to your partner's expectations and work toward a compromise. This will help build a healthy relationship built on mutual respect and trust.

## HOW TO SET HEALTHY EXPECTATIONS FOR YOURSELF

Setting healthy expectations for yourself is a crucial aspect of achieving success, maintaining balance, and preserving your well-being. When you have unrealistic or unhealthy expectations, it can lead to feelings of disappointment or failure, which can have a negative impact on your mental or physical health. Therefore, it's essential to learn how to establish healthy expectations to support your self-growth while keeping yourself out of harm's way.

Below, we will explore the importance of setting healthy expectations for yourself, along with tips to help you establish and maintain them.

- Determine your expectations: Before jumping into a new project or goal, take the time to determine your expectations. Are they realistic and achievable, or are they based on unrealistic standards? By setting achievable and realistic expectations from the start, you will prevent disappointment later on.
- Practice positive self-talk: Self-doubt and negative self-talk can lead to unhealthy expectations and prevent you from achieving your goals. By replacing negative self-talk with positive affirmations, you can boost your confidence and motivation, which can ultimately help you establish healthy expectations.
- Let go: Letting go of negative thoughts, beliefs, and expectations is vital to achieving self-growth. Learning to forgive yourself and release negative expectations and patterns can help you move forward and focus on positive movement.

- Change your mindset: A positive mindset is key when it comes to establishing healthy expectations. By changing your thoughts and reframing your mindset, you can shift your focus from limiting beliefs and expectations to positive and achievable goals.
- Focus on your accomplishments: When you focus on your accomplishments, you build your confidence and self-esteem to continue on a positive track. Evaluating what you've achieved and how you got there, and celebrating these accomplishments can help you focus on a more positive perspective and set healthy expectations.
- Know your limits: While setting challenging goals is significant, it's essential to know your limits. Pushing past your limits can result in burnout, which can hold you back from achieving future goals. Setting mental, physical, and emotional boundaries will help you avoid burnout and maintain balance in your life.
- Stay true to yourself: It's important to always stay true to your values, beliefs, and identity. Unrealistic expectations based on society's standards, or someone else's goals aren't serving your health and lead to negative mental or physical health outcomes.
- Practice gratitude: Practicing gratitude daily can help you maintain a positive outlook and focus on what's important. Feeling grateful for what you have in life

lets you appreciate and set meaningful goals rather than chase endless unrealistic expectations.

- Improve your self-confidence: Building self-confidence and self-esteem takes time and positive reinforcement. Surrounding yourself with positive and encouraging people, taking time to invest in yourself and learn new skills, and overcoming negative self-talk are effective ways to improve self-confidence.

By following these tips to set and maintain healthy expectations and reframing your mindset and habits toward a positive movement, you're well on your way to achieving self-growth, balance in your life, and improved mental and physical health outcomes. Remember, developing healthy expectations will enable you to set goals that are challenging but realistic, paving the road to personal success and achieving long-term secure relationships.

## HOW TO SET HEALTHY EXPECTATIONS IN YOUR RELATIONSHIP

Relationships are an essential part of life, from intimate relationships with your partners and family to professional relationships with colleagues and bosses. In any relationship, setting healthy expectations is crucial to establishing a strong foundation that leads to mutual understanding and a successful partnership.

Healthy expectations are those that are fair, reasonable, and align with your values and beliefs. They include open communication, respect for one another, mutual support, compromising, and agreeing on what behavior is healthy for you and your partner. For example, a healthy expectation in any relationship is to establish open and honest communication that will promote trust and respect. Some examples of healthy expectations in a relationship include:

- respectful conversations and open dialogue
- setting boundaries concerning what is acceptable and unacceptable behavior
- agreeing to disagree without judgment or resentment
- investing in quality time together regularly
- being supportive and understanding of each other's feelings
- taking responsibility for your own actions
- encouraging each other to reach personal and professional goals
- working together toward common goals

It's important to differentiate between healthy and unhealthy expectations in a relationship. Unhealthy expectations are often egocentric and may not be based on clear communication between partners. They can be emotionally damaging and lead to resentment and conflict within the relationship. For example, it is unhealthy to expect your partner to make decisions on your behalf without your input or approval. Some more examples of unhealthy expectations include:

- putting your partner down or belittling them
- abusive behavior or language
- forcing your beliefs and values on your partner
- controlling or manipulating your partner's behavior
- expecting your partner to take care of all the household tasks
- refusing to compromise or discuss issues

## MANAGING HEALTHY EXPECTATIONS

Setting and maintaining healthy expectations in a relationship can be difficult, but it is essential for a relationship to thrive. When navigating relationships and aligning them with your attachment style, it is essential to encourage healthy expectations. To achieve this, there are a few crucial factors to consider.

Firstly, communicate regularly with your partner to make sure you're both on the same page. Talk about specific expectations and ensure that you are clear and concise with your message. Avoid making assumptions, as it can lead to misunderstandings and frustration.

It's also essential not to compare your relationship to others. Every partnership is unique and has its own set of expectations and dynamics. Comparing your partnership to others may lead to unrealistic expectations that cannot be met, leading to frustration or disappointment.

Being realistic about your partner's capabilities is also crucial. Don't expect them to be perfect or to fulfill every want and need. Being aware of your partner's strengths and limitations can help you establish realistic expectations that benefit both of you.

Another critical aspect of managing expectations is taking care of yourself. Your relationship should not be the only area of your life that is important. As discussed in Steps 11 & 12, set time aside to pursue your interests, engage in activities that make you happy, and surround yourself with people who support and encourage you.

Space is also important in any type of relationship. However, in any partnership, allowing each other time and space to be themselves without feeling suffocated is vital. By providing space, you give your partner the freedom to be themselves, which can lead to a healthier, happier relationship.

Finally, be open-minded and willing to embrace change. Your partnership will evolve over time, and your expectations may change. Be flexible and willing to adapt to new situations that arise in your relationship.

JOURNAL PROMPTS

- Reflect on past experiences: Examine your past relationships and attachment patterns. How have your previous experiences shaped your expectations in relationships?
- What are the essential elements that contribute to your sense of security, trust, and emotional well-being? How can you communicate these needs effectively to your partner?
- Create a basic list of expectations you want to set for your current or future partner.
- Keep adding to the list as you remember what you desire. This list will come in handy later when it comes time to talk to your partner.
- How open are you to compromising on certain expectations to promote a harmonious and secure attachment?

Setting expectations might seem overwhelming or even selfish. However, having healthy expectations is like setting healthy standards—it's not too much, but just right to protect you from yourself, other people, and potentially devastating relationships. To take this a step further, we're going to dive into how to create healthy relationship goals.

15

# STEP 15: SET YOUR RELATIONSHIP GOALS

---

*We work hard on this relationship every day.*

— ANONYMOUS

---

Goals differ from expectations in that they are specific, measurable, and achievable. They also need to be relevant to your relationship and should be created collaboratively with your partner. The great part, though, is that you can, if you want, use some of your expectations to create goals. For instance, if you expect each other to be communicative about your feelings, then a goal could be to spend 30 minutes each day discussing how you're feeling and addressing any issues that have come up.

Take some time to think about what you want out of this relationship and how you can reasonably reach that goal. In this chapter, we're going to work on turning those visions and expectations into achievable goals.

## IS IT OKAY TO SET RELATIONSHIP GOALS?

Relationships are an integral part of our lives, and they can be an endless source of happiness and fulfillment if we nurture them with care and intention. One of the best ways to foster a secure and deep connection with your partner is by setting relationship goals. In this section, we will delve into the importance of setting relationship goals and why it is healthy for you and your partner to set goals regularly.

First and foremost, setting relationship goals while keeping your attachment styles in mind allows you and your partner to align your visions and aspirations for your relationship. You both get to define your shared values, expectations, and hopes for your future together. It helps you both to work toward a common aim and enables you to develop a shared sense of purpose in your relationship. Setting these goals can help you prioritize things that matter to you as a couple, allowing you to create more meaningful experiences, memories and build stronger connections.

In addition to providing a shared roadmap, setting relationship goals helps build trust and deepen intimacy in your relationship. By being open and honest about the things you both desire and aspire to achieve, you develop a deeper understanding and appreciation for each other. When you work together to accomplish these goals, it strengthens your bond and helps you both learn more about each other and recognize each other's strengths, weaknesses, and communication styles, which will make your relationship more resilient.

Another critical benefit of setting relationship goals is that it promotes self-reflection and personal growth, which are healthy for both the individual and the relationship. As you focus on your relationship objectives, you will become more aware of your personal strengths and limitations, which will lead to increased self-awareness and enhanced self-confidence. Furthermore, the goals you set for your relationship will challenge you and help you develop new skills as you work to accomplish them.

Setting small, achievable relationship goals can support incremental growth, build momentum, and engender a sense of satisfaction, which can encourage you to continue pushing forward and taking on bigger challenges as they come. When you and your partner achieve your goals together, it can create a sense of shared accomplishment, which deepens your emotional connection and supports a secure attachment.

216 | LEIGH W. HART

## HOW TO SET RELATIONSHIP GOALS

Setting healthy relationship goals is crucial for various reasons. It helps to build trust, increase intimacy, reduce conflicts, and promote healthier communication. When you set healthy relationship goals, you and your partner create a framework for how you want your relationship to be. Goals also allow you to focus on the things that matter most and work toward them together. Here are some tips on how to set and achieve healthy relationship goals.

Fight the problem, not the person: Arguments are inevitable in any relationship, but it's crucial to fight the problem, not the person. When you focus on attacking the issue rather than blaming your partner, you'll come up with solutions and ways to prevent the problem from recurring. For instance, instead of saying, "You are always so insensitive," consider saying, "It hurts me when you forget our plans." This way, your partner won't feel attacked or go on the defensive.

- You can accomplish this by talking through the issues and working together to come up with solutions that work for both of you. You can also agree to take a timeout whenever you feel like an argument is about to begin or schedule regular check-ins.

Communicate effectively: Communication is the foundation of every great relationship. Setting a goal to communicate more effectively will help you and your partner discuss your feelings and thoughts in a healthier way. Instead of shutting down, yelling, or bringing up unrelated subjects, practice active listening and try to understand each other's perspectives. Remember to be clear and concise when communicating, and avoid making assumptions.

- A good way to do this is by setting aside time each week to discuss your relationship and set intentions. Stay away from using labels or accusations when addressing issues. Instead, use "I" statements and focus on your feelings and needs. For example, instead of saying, "You are so lazy," you could say, "I feel like I'm carrying the load in this relationship." An easy way to accomplish this goal is by practicing mindfulness and pausing before reacting.

Make up after fights: Arguments happen, but it's essential to make up after them. Setting a goal to reconcile after a fight can improve your relationship and prevent grudges. Apologize when necessary, and forgive your partner. Create an after-fight ritual like cuddling, watching a movie, or taking a walk together.

- To accomplish this, take the time to talk through each other's grievances after a fight. Also, try to focus

on finding common ground and understanding
where your partner is coming from instead of
attacking them. As a couple, you can also decide not
to go to bed angry or set aside at least one date night
per month.

Practice radical openness and honesty: Honesty is essential
in any relationship. Setting a goal to practice radical open-
ness and honesty means being truthful without being cruel.
It's about telling your partner the truth without hiding
anything or omitting details. Be respectful and approach
sensitive topics with sensitivity.

- You can do this by creating an open line of
  communication with your partner and discussing
  difficult topics when necessary. You can also practice
  vulnerability without fear of judgment or criticism.
  To ensure you do this, you can set aside time each
  week for meaningful conversations and being
  honest, even if it is uncomfortable.

Have more fun: Relationships are not always about serious
talks and responsibilities; it's essential to have fun too. Set a
goal to prioritize fun and laughter in your relationship. Try
new hobbies together, plan a day trip or vacation, or play
games together.

- By making time for leisure activities and getting out of your comfort zone, you can have more fun with your partner. Be creative with the way you spend time together. Easy ways to accomplish this goal are by planning regular date nights or weekend getaways or by simply taking a few minutes each day to laugh together. These tips will help you set and achieve healthy relationship goals.

Improve your sex life: Sex is a crucial aspect of a healthy partnership. Setting a goal to improve your sexual life ensures that you and your partner feel satisfied and connected emotionally and physically. Be open to exploring new techniques and trying new things. Talk about your desires and preferences, and be willing to listen to your partner too.

- Don't be afraid to talk openly about sex and experiment with different activities. Practice communication and build trust by setting aside time for intimate conversations or trying something new each month.

Invest in the relationship regularly: Relationships need consistent effort and work. Setting a goal to invest regularly in the relationship means setting aside time and resources to nurture it. It could mean planning surprise dates, cooking your partner's favorite meal, or giving compliments regularly.

- You can accomplish this by building a foundation of trust and understanding. Practice being selfless and be prepared to make sacrifices for your partner. Easy ways to do this are by thanking each other for small gestures or acts of kindness, or simply reminding yourself why you're in the relationship.

Grow and build together: Relationships shouldn't stagnate. They require growth and development. Setting a goal to grow and build together means embracing new challenges, learning together, and supporting each other through life's ups and downs.

- Do this by focusing on self-improvement and working toward shared goals. Practice compassion and show your partner you care, even when things get challenging. You can also try attending classes together, reading inspiring books, or taking turns motivating each other. These tips will help you set and achieve healthy relationship goals.

Learn and understand each other's love languages: Love languages refer to the various ways people experience and express love. Knowing and understanding your partner's love language can help you communicate love in a way that is most effective for them. Take a quiz or read a book on love languages, and discuss your results with your partner.

- Accomplish this by being open to learning and expressing yourself in new ways. Be patient and willing to give each other time and space if needed. Also, by creating acts of service specific to your partner's love language or simply taking the time to truly listen when they speak, you can engage more in their love language.

Have a weekly date night: Life can get hectic, and it can be challenging to prioritize your relationship with busy schedules. Setting a goal to have a weekly date night allows you and your partner to reconnect and focus on each other. Plan the date night together and make it a time to enjoy each other's company without distractions.

- You can ensure you do this by preparing ahead of time and being intentional about the way you spend your time. Set reminders in your calendar, or simply take turns deciding where you'll go each week.

## JOURNAL PROMPTS

- If you are single, write out goals for your future relationship.
- If you are in a relationship, write out goals you would like to strive for now for you and your partner.
- Keep this list handy because it will help with the next step.

Assuming you worked through the journal prompts in each chapter, you should now have a list of your boundaries, expectations, and goals. However, the question remains: how can you effectively convey these concerns to your partner, family, and friends? In the upcoming chapter, we will explore invaluable strategies that will empower you to navigate these conversations with clarity and mutual understanding.

# 16

# STEP 16: IT'S TIME TO TALK

*Love is supposed to be based on trust, and trust on love, it's something rare and beautiful when people can confide in each other without fearing what the other person will think.*

— E.A. BUCCHIANERI

In any type of relationship, communication is key. But for those with an insecure attachment type, sharing your thoughts and feelings can be a challenge. It's easy to feel overwhelmed and shut down, leading to misunderstandings and unmet expectations. That's why it's important to work on opening up, especially in a romantic relationship.

## OPENING UP TO YOUR PARTNER

Opening up means being vulnerable and honest about your thoughts and feelings. It involves sharing your hopes, fears, dreams, and desires with your partner. By doing so, you create a deeper level of intimacy and trust, allowing you both to feel seen and heard in the relationship. The more you share with each other, the more you'll feel connected and supported.

Opening up can also help you avoid misunderstandings and conflicts. When you communicate what you do and don't want, you set clear expectations for your partner. This allows them to better understand your needs and helps them be more responsive to your desires. By having open and honest communication, you create a safe space for both you and your partner to express yourselves freely without any fear of judgment.

Here's an example: Let's say you're in a committed relationship, and you've been feeling distant from your partner lately. Rather than shutting down and keeping your feelings to yourself, you decide to open up. You express how you're feeling and what you need to feel more connected. By doing so, you're creating an opportunity for your partner to understand your needs and make an effort to meet them.

In closing, opening up is crucial for any relationship to succeed. Whether or not you have an insecure attachment type, sharing your thoughts and feelings with your partner can help create a deeper level of understanding and intimacy. It's important to communicate what you want and don't want so that everyone is on the same page. The more you open up, the more you'll feel seen and heard, ultimately leading to a happier and healthier relationship.

### *What to Open Up to Your Partner About*

Opening up to your partner is an essential aspect of any healthy relationship. It is important to note that sharing your deepest thoughts and feelings with your partner is not something that comes easy for everyone, but it is worth the effort. The foundation of a healthy relationship is built on trust, understanding, and effective communication, so sharing your innermost thoughts and feelings with your partner can help establish these fundamental principles.

One of the most crucial topics to consider discussing with your partner is your triggers. By sharing your triggers with your partner, they can better understand how to approach particular topics or situations with you. This can help to avoid unnecessary conflicts and misunderstandings, which can damage the relationship. For example, if a trigger for you is feeling like your partner isn't being honest with you, it's helpful to share that trigger with them so that they can be more aware of it and take steps to address it in the future.

Another relevant topic to discuss with your partner is expectations. When starting a relationship, both parties inevitably have some expectations that they want to be met. These expectations can range from how often you communicate with each other to what you expect from your partner in terms of emotional support. Discussing your expectations and finding a way to compromise is important for both parties, as it can help prevent disappointment and disillusionment later on. If an expectation you have is not being met, it can be beneficial to discuss why and how you can work together to meet that expectation in the future.

Boundaries are another topic that you can consider discussing with your partner. Discussing boundaries with your partner allows them to respect your space and ensures that both parties feel comfortable with the relationship's pace. It also helps to create a sense of trust between the two of you, which is essential for any healthy relationship. Boundaries will differ for everyone, but if a boundary for you is not being pushed to do something you don't feel comfortable with or not being judged for your beliefs, it can be helpful to communicate these expectations with your partner.

Talking about your goals is also essential in a relationship. Sharing your short-term and long-term goals with your partner can allow them to understand what you want to achieve in life and how they fit into the picture. This can help you both work towards a common goal and support each other in achieving your dreams. For instance, if your goal is to get a higher education, discussing this with your partner can help them understand why you might dedicate a lot of time to your studies and how they can support you.

Additionally, anything you think applies to your personal growth or the growth of the relationship should be discussed. Talking about your opinions, beliefs, and values can help to keep the relationship honest and healthy, as it encourages both parties to stay true to themselves. This may include topics such as religion, money, and lifestyle choices.

When you do have these conversations, be willing to listen to and accept your partner's triggers, boundaries, expectations, and goals as well. A fulfilling relationship takes effort from both partners. If you discover your expectations and goals are not in alignment, you can discuss ways to find common ground. And if you are in a new relationship, this may be the discussion that helps you determine if this is a healthy relationship that you should continue to pursue.

### How to Open Up to Your Partner

Opening up and being vulnerable can be scary, but it's crucial for a secure relationship. When you share your thoughts, feelings, and experiences with your partner, you build a deeper level of trust and intimacy. It can also help identify any issues that need to be addressed within the relationship.

Here are some tips on how to open up to your partner:

- If you need a good icebreaker, refer back to the "relationship check-in" questions from Step 8 for ideas.
- Talking compassionately and non-accusingly whenever you're triggered: It's easy to lash out or become defensive when you're feeling hurt or angry, but it's important to take a deep breath and talk through the situation calmly and compassionately. Try to focus on understanding each other's perspective instead of assigning blame or judgment.
- Learning how to compromise: It's an essential part of any relationship. Compromising means finding a solution that works for both people and being willing to give and take as needed. It requires understanding, patience, and a willingness to listen to each other's needs.
- Create a safe and open environment where everyone feels free to be themselves: This means respecting each other's boundaries and values, and listening without judgment. It also means being willing to talk about difficult topics in a kind and non-confrontational way.
- Be open to sharing all feelings—even the ugly ones: It's important to be honest and open about all of your feelings, both positive and negative. This can

help create a safe space for both of you to be vulnerable and foster a stronger connection.

- Be open to your partner's help: It's okay to ask for help or admit that you need it. Doing so can help your partner understand and support you better, which can strengthen the bond between you.

- Refrain from retreating: When things get tough, it's easy to want to retreat and shut down. However, this can create distance between both of you. Instead, try to work through the problem together and find ways to make it better.

- Remember that you deserve love no matter what: It's important to remember that even when things get hard, you deserve love and respect. That means loving yourself and your partner, no matter what.

- Listen as much as you talk: In any relationship, it's important to make sure both people feel heard. Take the time to really listen to your partner and respond in a way that shows you both care about each other.

- Show appreciation: Showing gratitude and expressing appreciation for your partner is a great way to build a strong bond. Acknowledging the things your partner does for you can help create a deeper connection and foster trust.

- Don't be afraid to make mistakes, and allow them to make mistakes too: Mistakes are part of life and relationships. Acknowledging them and learning

230 | LEIGH W. HART

from them can help bring you closer together in the long run.

## HOW TO OPEN UP TO YOUR FAMILY

Opening up with your family members is an essential part of building close relationships and maintaining healthy communication. It can be challenging to share your thoughts, feelings, and worries with your family, but keeping things bottled up can cause emotional stress, affect your mental health, and create unwanted tension. Now that you have a better understanding of your attachment style, here's why opening up with your family is important and how you can communicate healthy boundaries without feeling guilty or overwhelmed.

Firstly, when you open up, you give your family the opportunity to understand you better. This creates empathy, and they can feel what you're feeling, understand your situation better, and offer support when you need it. For instance, if you're struggling with anxiety, talking to your parents or siblings about it can help them recognize your triggers, and they may offer support by taking up activities with you that may help you relax.

Secondly, opening up with your family members can strengthen your relationships with them. When you're open, honest, and share your struggles with them, it makes them feel valued and appreciated. By creating an atmosphere of trust, you'll encourage them to open up to you too, giving you a better understanding of who they are and what they may be going through. This creates a deeper connection and strengthens your bond with your family members.

### How to Communicate Boundaries With Your Family

Now, let's talk about communicating healthy boundaries. It's important to have boundaries in all relationships to ensure mutual respect and protect your well-being. When setting boundaries, it's essential to communicate them with kindness and compassion. For example, you may opt to stay over with your parents every Saturday night, but only up to a certain time so that you can get enough rest for the following day. You can let them know in a loving way that you need to catch up on sleep and that leaving at that time is best for your mental health.

Communicating boundaries with your family can be challenging and uncomfortable, but it's essential for your mental and emotional well-being. Here are some effective ways to communicate boundaries with your family.

### Role Play

One effective way to set boundaries with your family is through role-playing. This means practicing what you will say or do in response to a common situation that usually triggers a boundary violation. For instance, if your parents always show up unannounced, you can practice what you'll say the next time they do so. By role-playing, you gain confidence and clarity when it comes to communicating boundaries.

## Write It Out

If you're not comfortable with role-playing, another way to communicate boundaries with your family is by writing them out. Take some time to think about what specific boundaries you'd like to set and write them down. Once you've written them down, it's easier to communicate them to your family. Make sure you're clear and concise when communicating your boundaries.

## Talk to Others

Talking to other family members or friends can be helpful when it comes to communicating boundaries. They can act as your support system and offer advice and guidance on how to deal with your family. It's crucial to talk to people outside your family circle, as they can offer an objective perspective.

## Value Your Time and Ask Others to Do the Same

Setting boundaries means valuing your time and asking others to respect it as well. If you have work or other commitments, let your family know that you won't be available at certain times. Make sure you communicate this clearly, so they don't feel ignored or neglected.

## Be Direct but Kind

When communicating boundaries, it's important to be direct and clear about your needs. At the same time, be gentle and kind in your approach. Remember, you're not trying to hurt anyone's feelings or cause conflict. Instead, you're taking care of yourself, and that's a responsible thing to do.

## Avoid Engaging in Gossip

Gossip is never healthy, especially within a family. Avoid talking about other family members behind their backs or engaging in negative conversations. When you communicate boundaries, make sure you're not being judgmental or critical of others. Instead, focus on your needs and how you can communicate them effectively.

## Be Realistic in Your Expectations

Setting boundaries with your family can take time and effort. It's essential to be patient and realistic in your expectations. Your family may not understand or agree with your boundaries immediately. Don't get discouraged; keep communicating and reiterating them until they become a part of your family dynamic.

## Avoid Social Media or Any Other Triggers

Finally, be mindful of any triggers that can make it difficult to set boundaries. For example, if social media interactions with your family are causing anxiety, limit your social media use or consider deleting your accounts. Similarly, avoid any other triggers that can make it harder to maintain boundaries.

## HOW TO OPEN UP TO YOUR FRIENDS

Opening up to friends is an essential part of building and maintaining secure relationships. However, sharing personal information can be daunting, especially if you fear being judged or rejected. But, when we do not share our thoughts and emotions, we deprive ourselves of the benefits of friendship, such as receiving emotional support and guidance.

The importance of opening up to friends can be seen in the numerous benefits you can gain from it. When you share your emotions and feelings with friends, it helps to reduce stress and anxiety. It can also strengthen your bond with your friends, as they will feel closer to you and appreciate your trust in them. Additionally, sharing your thoughts and feelings can help you gain different perspectives, forming a more personalized and insightful solution to your problems.

That said, while opening up to your friends is vital, communicating healthy boundaries with your attachment style in mind is equally important. While it's easy to blur the lines between sharing and oversharing, learning how to communicate healthy boundaries is crucial for maintaining a healthy and happy friendship.

Here are some essential techniques for communicating healthy boundaries with friends:

- Be clear about what you are willing to share: It is essential to know what you want to share before opening up to your friends. Knowing your emotional limits will help you communicate your needs explicitly, avoiding unintended oversharing.

- Express your intentions early on: Let your friends know your intentions beforehand. Communicating your purpose or the reason for sharing with your friends will help prevent any confusion or misunderstanding that could lead to miscommunication.

- Be clear about your limits: Before you open up, talk to your friend about the specific limits you would like to set. Specify how much information you are willing to share and what personal boundaries your friend should not cross.

- Listen to your intuition: Always listen to your gut feelings when it comes to sharing personal information. If something feels off, it probably is, so take a step back, reconsider, and communicate with your friend to set appropriate boundaries.

- Find the right person: Share your story with close friends and family members that you trust. Avoid sharing personal information with people who might not understand or respect your boundaries.

- Focus on how you feel: When you open up, focus on how you feel and avoid blaming or attacking your friends. Talk about the emotions that the situation has stirred in you rather than placing judgment or criticism on others.

- Ask for what you need: When you're discussing a situation with your friends, make it clear what kind of support or advice you need. Doing so will help them better understand how they can help you.

By using these techniques, you can feel safe and supported in your friendships without sacrificing your mental and emotional health. Ultimately, building and maintaining healthy relationships involves respecting and valuing each other's boundaries, allowing for growth in the relationship.

## JOURNAL PROMPTS

Don't go into any conversation unprepared. Your journal pages are full of notes you can use to gather your thoughts.

- Create a list of people you would like to speak to and what about.
- After referring to your journal notes, write down boundaries, expectations, and goals for each relationship that are important to you.
- Write down compromises or changes that you are willing to make to satisfy your relationships.
- Which specific communication skills or strategies discussed in this chapter do you believe will bring the greatest value when it comes time to

communicate your boundaries, expectations, and goals with your partner, family, and friends?

When you feel ready, start addressing each person on your list and talking to them about your newfound self.

Opening up to your partner, family, and friends may not always come easy, but the rewards from having tough conversations are significant. It's possible that you may have been hesitant to initiate these conversations in the past, but you are now better equipped to handle them. Understanding your attachment style and how it influences your triggers and impacts your relationships has helped you identify the boundaries, expectations, and goals that are most beneficial for you. Do you know how powerful this newfound self-awareness can be? With this knowledge, you can confidently communicate needs that are customized to your specific situation to your loved ones and friends in a way that will benefit both you and your relationships.

# 17

# STEP 17: REGROUP, RESET, AND CONTINUE HEALING

*Vulnerability sounds like truth and feels like courage. Truth and courage aren't always comfortable, but they're never weakness.*

— BRENÉ BROWN

This chapter assesses your progress and determines how you can continue healing, so before you continue reading, go to your journal and reread what you've written. Evaluating your progress is an integral part of personal growth, and by reflecting on the lessons you've learned, you'll be in a better position to move forward. Once you've read through your journal and reflected on the topics that resonated with you, move on to the "Regroup and Reset" section. Here, you'll explore various ways of managing your emotions and continuing on the path of healing. Remember, you are in charge of your own healing journey.

## REGROUP AND RESET

Regrouping and resetting are crucial parts of the healing process. It's important to take time for yourself to refocus, recharge, and revitalize. This allows you to come back to the process feeling refreshed, motivated, and ready to continue. Consider the following tips for managing your emotions and regrouping.

### *Assessing Your Own Progress*

Assessing our progress is an incredibly important aspect of healing and developing healthy attachment styles. It allows us to take stock of our progress, determine what is and is not working, and make adjustments as necessary. Being able to recognize where we have improved and where we still need to work is a critical factor in our ability to move forward in life. In this section, we'll explore why it's important to assess progress and provide a detailed look at the methods you can use to determine and assess your progress toward healing and developing a secure attachment style.

## Why It's Important to Assess Progress

Knowing where you stand is an important part of the healing process. Without assessing your progress, it can be challenging to know if what you're doing is working or not. Assessment can provide clarity around what works and what doesn't, enabling better decision-making going forward. Assessing progress gives you a sense of control over your healing process, providing an opportunity to celebrate milestones achieved and progress made.

## Methods to Determine and Assess Progress

There are many techniques you can use to become more self-aware and assess your progress along the way. Here are some examples:

Focus on outcome measures instead of process measures: When assessing progress, focusing on the outcome measures can help you get a better idea of your growth. Instead of looking at how many therapy sessions you've had, take a look at what you've accomplished during those sessions. Have you changed your relationships? Have you been able to overcome problematic habits or behaviors? Assess the final outcome and what it means for your overall healing journey.

- If you've been in therapy for six months, instead of looking at the number of sessions, consider what changes have been made in that time. Have you built healthier relationships? Have you been able to better regulate your emotions or make progress in other areas? Ask yourself thought-provoking questions to get a better sense of your progress.

Improved boundaries: Improving boundaries is a significant indicator of development that should be celebrated. If you're working toward developing a secure attachment style, improved personal boundaries are a great indicator of progress. Setting clearer and healthier boundaries means you're becoming more secure within yourself and in relationships, a major milestone in the healing process.

- Take a moment to consider: Do you feel less anxious and more in control when interacting with people? Are you better able to express your needs in relationships and not compromise yourself?

Completed goals: Setting goals can be helpful in determining progress. If you've been working on a personal or professional goal, assess whether or not you've made progress toward that goal, even if the objective hasn't been completely achieved yet. Successfully setting a goal and taking steps to achieve it indicates progress.

- For instance, if one of your goals is to start a business, consider what steps have been taken toward that goal. Have you done research? Have you taken classes or read books related to the venture?

Setting and achieving goals can provide more clarity around how much progress you've made in your healing journey.

Reduced symptoms: Many times, our attachment issues can manifest in various symptoms such as anxiety or depression. Improvement in these symptoms can indicate that you're making progress toward healing. When assessing progress, keep track of these changes and seek professional help if necessary.

- If you've been dealing with anxiety, track how often and how intensely it appears throughout your healing process. Have there been any days where the anxiety was particularly low? Are there certain activities or strategies that have helped reduce the symptoms? Monitoring these changes can provide insight into the progress made. By assessing progress, we can celebrate milestones achieved and become more self-aware of our healing journey.

Increased self-trust: Improved self-trust is another important indicator of progress. When we're struggling with attachment issues, it can be hard to trust ourselves and others. Working on this aspect of our lives can have a significant impact. If you find yourself taking more risks or relying more on yourself, take note of how far you've come.

- For instance, if you've been participating in therapy and working on building self-trust, assess how often you turn to yourself for validation or guidance. Have there been instances where it felt easier to trust your own intuition? These changes can be an indication of progress.

Increased emotional intelligence: Developing higher emotional intelligence can help us navigate our relationships and emotions more effectively. When working on developing our emotional intelligence, it's helpful to track our progress over time. Assessing your progress in this area may involve identifying your emotions more accurately, being more empathetic toward others, or responding better in emotionally charged situations.

- Consider: Are you able to read people's body language more accurately or better recognize your own emotional triggers? These are all signs that you're making progress in learning how to better understand and manage emotions.

## REFLECTING ON YOUR GROWTH

- Have you been writing your thoughts daily?
- Have you continued to recognize triggers?
- Are you following your own boundaries?
- Are you still dreaming about your goals?
- Are you still practicing self-care?
- Are you still using positive mantras and breathing techniques?
- Did you communicate with your partner, family, and friends?

### *Celebrate Your Small Wins and Milestones*

Assessing your progress is essential to helping you stay motivated and continually improve. It provides you with a clear understanding of where you currently are and where you need to be. It is beneficial to regularly reflect on your journey and give yourself credit for the progress you've made.

One way to assess your progress is to use the concept of marginal gains. This concept was popularized by the British cycling team, which used it to achieve remarkable success in the Tour de France. Marginal gains are a series of small improvements that, when combined, lead to significant progress.

Marginal gains are an important tool because they help you identify areas where you can make small, incremental improvements. Focusing on small improvements that add up over time helps make progress feel more achievable and manageable. It also means that you're much more likely to maintain momentum and stay motivated toward achieving your goals.

From here, you can celebrate your small wins and set goals for the future. The key is to stay focused on your journey and to note the progress that you make, however small it may be. This will help ensure that you keep making positive changes and continue along the road to success.

For instance, if you want to improve your attachment in your relationship, you could set specific goals such as scheduling more dates or making time for regular conversations. Celebrate each step toward this goal and make a note of how far you've come—this will help keep the process enjoyable and meaningful.

Celebrating small wins is crucial for improving our attachment style, as it helps foster positive emotions and a sense of self-worth. Here are five effective ways to celebrate small wins:

- Reward yourself: It is a well-known fact that rewards boost our motivation to succeed. Set up some small rewards for yourself before working on any task, and when you accomplish them, treat yourself to something that you genuinely enjoy. It could be anything from indulging in some ice cream or shopping for something small to binge-watching your favorite show. These rewards will help you associate a positive emotion with your success, and thus, reinforce your attachment to positive experiences.

- Simply notice: it's easy to overlook small successes in our day-to-day lives. Therefore, make an effort to consciously recognize these small wins. This can mean taking the time to appreciate moments that make you feel happy, even if they seem minor. Acknowledging a small success can help build your self-esteem and attachment style, as it creates positive feelings within you.

- Get excited: When something goes well, embrace that feeling of excitement! Allow yourself to feel joy over the small wins you accomplish, even if they seem insignificant. Excitement and joy trigger the reward system in our brain, which helps form strong attachment bonds. So, whether you did well on a test or a presentation, take a moment to feel that excitement and celebrate the win.

- Be present: Mindfulness is a beneficial practice for recognizing and celebrating small wins. Mindfulness allows us to be fully present at the moment without judgment, enabling us to appreciate each moment fully. Celebrating small wins through mindfulness involves taking a moment to relish in your success and examining your emotions, thoughts, and sensations about the experience.

- Be compassionate toward yourself: Perfect is an ideal that we all aspire to, which can, at times, be overwhelming. Self-compassion toward ourselves is crucial when celebrating small wins. When we do something well, we have to give ourselves the gift of self-care instead of getting stuck in self-judgment for not doing something "*perfectly*." Compassion helps build resilience and makes us more resistant to challenges.

Reflecting on the lessons learned, no matter how big or small, is an important part of personal growth. To be able to truly celebrate small wins and make progress, it's important to stay mindful and self-compassionate. Taking the time to honor your successes and reflect on the lessons learned will foster motivation, invigorate relationships, and open up new possibilities.

## JOURNAL PROMPTS

- What was the most important lesson you learned from this book?
- Reflect on a recent accomplishment or milestone that you are proud of. How did it make you feel? What challenges did you overcome to achieve it?

- List three small wins or positive moments that you experienced recently. How did these moments contribute to your overall well-being or progress?
- What positive changes have you noticed in your relationships?
- How did it feel to overcome a recent challenge?
- Take a moment to appreciate the journey you have been on so far. Write a letter to yourself acknowledging the progress you have made, the obstacles you have overcome, and the milestones you have reached. Reading this letter in the future, whether it's in one month, six months, or even one year, will have a profound impact.

## CONTINUE HEALING

We are not done growing, learning, or healing. We might be adults in relationships with bills to pay and kids to take care of, but that does not mean our development as people has to stop. Working on and improving your insecure attachment style can be done in any phase of life. It requires a commitment to oneself and a desire for personal growth. Following are a few tips to help you continue healing and growing.

### Don't Keep Yourself From Being Social

Social interaction is a vital component of our mental and physical well-being. Humans are social beings, and without social interactions, we often struggle to lead fulfilling and healthy lives. Studies have shown that socialization is crucial for a wide range of emotional and physical issues. It can help reduce stress, anxiety, depression and even improve our immune system. Furthermore, social interaction also plays a crucial role in helping people heal their insecure attachment styles.

Fortunately, social interaction can help people with insecure attachment styles improve their relationships. Positive interactions with others may lead to an increased sense of trust and improved communication skills. Engaging in healthy and productive relationships can help people with insecure attachment styles feel more secure and loved.

For those looking to improve their social interactions, there are many small and comfortable activities that they can do. Some examples include joining a social club, volunteering at a local organization, taking a class or workshop, or even attending a social gathering or event. These activities can provide an excellent opportunity to meet new people, build friendships, and improve communication skills.

In particular, joining a social club or class related to an individual's interests can make socialization more comfortable and enjoyable. For instance, someone interested in writing could join a writing group, where they can find people who share similar hobbies and interests. This provides a natural and stress-free way to meet new people and expand social networks.

Volunteering in your local community is another great way to meet new people and enhance social interactions. Many organizations need volunteers, and the task can be a team-building exercise that allows people to work together and get to know each other better. It is a great way to meet people with shared interests and values.

In closing, social interaction plays a crucial role in keeping us healthy, happy, and fulfilled. It helps improve our mental and physical health as well as our attachment styles. Practicing small, comfortable activities that align with our interests can be a great way to improve our social interactions. Whether it is joining a social club, volunteering, or attending a gathering, taking steps to build positive and healthy relationships can have a significant impact on our lives.

### Keep Reading and Learning

Reading and learning are important for many reasons, especially when you're working on healing your insecure attachment style. Reading and delegated learning can help you reflect on your experiences, develop new perspectives and ideas, and gain insight into the deeper complexities of relationships. Furthermore, it provides a great way to process difficult feelings or emotions that come up in relationships. A variety of reading materials, such as books, articles, blogs, and even poems, can provide useful information and guidance on how to better understand yourself and others.

Some of the chapters in this book may have resonated more with you, than others. Some topics may need a little more reading and effort to truly sink in. There are some materials that may feel more challenging than others, but these can be beneficial in helping to stretch and expand your thinking. It's important to remember that reading and learning can help you heal your attachment style, but they are only pieces of the puzzle. Taking this knowledge and applying it by engaging in healthy relationships is also an important part of the process.

I encourage you to reread or do a deep dive into any materials that interest you. Reflect on your own experiences and relationships, then use the knowledge you've gained to create positive change in your life.

### The Importance of Seeking Professional Help

Seeking professional help is an important step toward a happier, healthier life. It can be easy to feel ashamed or embarrassed about seeking help, as though it means something is totally wrong with us. However, this couldn't be further from the truth. Mental health struggles are common, and seeking help is a sign of strength, not weakness.

There are many reasons why seeking professional help is so important. Firstly, a trained therapist has the knowledge and experience to help you work through your issues in a way that is effective and safe. Rather than relying on your own limited knowledge and experience, a counselor can provide you with tools and techniques that are proven to be effective.

Additionally, therapy provides a safe space for you to explore your thoughts and feelings without fear of judgment or shame. Sometimes, it's difficult to open up to friends or family members about the things that are causing us pain. A therapist, however, is there to listen and offer support without any preconceived notions or biases. This can be incredibly liberating and allow you to explore your own thoughts and feelings in greater detail.

Finally, therapy is a way to enhance the positive changes you've already made in your life. Many of the issues we face can be difficult to overcome on our own, and having a therapist guide us through the process can make all the difference. By working with a counselor, we can gain a deeper understanding of ourselves and our struggles and develop new strategies for overcoming the obstacles we face.

For those who are already in counseling, it's important to recognize and celebrate the progress you've made so far. Healing is a difficult journey, and it takes time and effort to get there. However, the benefits of therapy are immense, and by sticking with it, you are giving yourself the best possible chance to live a happy and fulfilling life.

Overall, seeking professional help is an important step toward healing and happiness. It's nothing to be ashamed of —in fact, it's a sign of strength and self-awareness. You've learned a lot of information throughout this book, and now it's time to start applying and integrating that knowledge. However, with a counselor, coach, or therapist by your side, you're more likely to stick to your changes—and succeed.

By working with a trained therapist, we can gain the tools and insights we need to live our best lives. So if you're feeling stuck or overwhelmed, don't hesitate to reach out for help. Remember that knowledge without action is useless, so don't just think about what you've read. Put it into practice, and let the power of personal growth work its magic.

## JOURNAL PROMPTS

- Make a list of social activities you would like to try. Set a goal for how many times a week or month you will prioritize social encounters.
- Of all the steps and topics covered in this book, which ones resonated with you the most? Search out additional reading materials to learn more about those specific topics.
- Are you in counseling already? Reflect on and write down what you have accomplished so far with your counselor. Then make a list of areas that you would like to continue working on.
- If you are not seeing a counselor, but would like to, what are the top five areas of concern you would like to bring up during your first appointment?

As you come to the end of this chapter, take a moment to appreciate the progress you have made on your healing journey. Recognize the value of regrouping, resetting, and continuing to nurture your well-being. Celebrate the small wins and milestones along the way, for they are significant markers of your growth. Remember to stay connected with others, engage in ongoing learning, and seek professional support if needed. With each step forward, you are empowering yourself to create a life filled with authentic, secure connections.

## Reach Out a Helping Hand to Someone Else

Your journey is just beginning... and that puts you in the perfect position to help someone else get started on theirs.

Simply by sharing your honest opinion of this book and your own experiences on Amazon, you'll show new readers where they can find everything they need to understand their attachment style – and use this understanding to build healthier and more secure relationships.

**TAKE A MOMENT TO SHARE YOUR THOUGHTS!**

Thank you so much for your support. We all need a helping hand from time to time, and I'm so happy to have you on board.

**Scan the QR code for a quick review!**

# CONCLUSION

---

*What happens when people open their hearts? They get better.*

— HARUKI MURAKAMI

---

Congratulations. You have completed *Don't Get Derailed by Your Attachment Style*. Now that you have gained a better understanding of your attachment style and how it affects your relationships, you can use this knowledge to more consciously create healthy, secure attachments with important people in your life.

Upon completing this book, creating more healthy connections might still seem overwhelming, and that's totally okay.

Remember, it takes time and patience to build secure attachments. But no matter what our attachment style is, we can all create loving bonds with those around us.

Expressing love and affection can be tough, even for people with secure attachments. They might worry about what others will think, or they might be anxious about being rejected. So the goal isn't to be completely worry free or fearless, but to begin the journey of creating connections and loving relationships with greater awareness. With self-awareness, patience, and trust in yourself, you can gradually build secure attachments with those around you.

And by understanding your attachment style, you can develop that self-awareness as you become more mindful of how it affects you and take steps toward forming healthier bonds. Now that you have the tools to start down this path, go ahead and give yourself permission to enjoy love in all its forms.

It's important to remember that your attachment style was formed from experiences in the past and doesn't need to stay the same forever. You can always work to develop healthy attachments with those around you. With an understanding of your own attachment style and a few simple changes in how you interact, you can create more meaningful relationships.

Here's a brief reminder of what you've learned:

There are four attachment styles: anxious, avoidant, fearful or disorganized, and secure.

If you have an anxious attachment style, you may feel easily overwhelmed by emotions and be overly sensitive to rejection.

- In relationships, an anxious attachment style can manifest as clinginess, overthinking, and obsessing. Some triggers may include a fear of abandonment or feeling neglected.
- To improve your anxious attachment style, you can: Externalize your feelings, reparent your inner child, or regulate your nervous system.

If you have an avoidant attachment style, you may struggle with vulnerability and push away emotional closeness.

- In relationships, an avoidant attachment style can manifest as an inability to trust, difficulty expressing emotions, and a need for control. Some triggers may include fear of intimacy and feeling suffocated.
- To improve your avoidant attachment style you can: Identify your avoidant strategies, distract yourself from intrusive thoughts, or create a relationship gratitude list.

A fearful or disorganized attachment can manifest itself in various ways, including feeling overwhelmed by feelings of anger or despair.

- In relationships, a fearful or disorganized attachment style can manifest as difficulty developing trust, feelings of shame and guilt, and a fear of vulnerability. Some triggers may include feeling invalidated or misunderstood.
- To improve your fearful or disorganized attachment style, you can: take a moment to pause and recalibrate, communicate effectively, or process your emotions in a healthy space.

Secure attachment is characterized by self-confidence, trust, mutual respect, and the ability to be present and connected in relationships.

- In relationships, a secure attachment style can manifest as the ability to communicate clearly and comfort others, seek support when needed, and feel comfortable with intimacy.
- To maintain your secure attachment style, you can: Practice self-care, set healthy boundaries, and be mindful of how your past affects your present.

Overall, when you're working on personal growth and inner healing, it's important to:

- recognize your patterns and triggers so you can work on them
- practice self-compassion and be mindful of your thoughts and emotions
- practice self-care so you can stay connected to yourself
- work on mental strengthening to handle difficult situations
- set healthy boundaries, expectations, and goals so you can stay connected to your values
- communicate effectively so others can understand you and your needs
- trust yourself and be willing to take risks in relationships
- regroup, reassess, and reset when needed so you can keep moving forward
- and lastly, give yourself permission to love and be loved in all its forms

With your newfound understanding of attachment styles, you can start to build healthier connections with those around you. By being compassionate toward yourself and others, while also striving for connection and authenticity in your relationships, you can create meaningful attachments that enrich your life and the lives of those around you, and I know this from personal experience.

For many years, I lived with PTSD and anxiety that kept me from connecting with others. I avoided social situations and found peace in being alone. But I knew that wasn't a healthy mindset to stay in because I ultimately wanted healthy connections with others. Recognizing that I wasn't sure why I chose to isolate myself, I knew I couldn't overcome this challenge on my own.

But, once I began to understand my avoidant attachment style and learned how to communicate more effectively with those around me, I started to form meaningful connections with people that fed my soul. I could finally find the support and understanding I needed from others so that I no longer kept myself isolated.

It took a lot of effort, but I learned to recognize my triggers and respond appropriately instead of reacting emotionally. Through therapy and self-reflection, I learned tools for managing my emotions, creating healthy boundaries, and fostering meaningful connections. And in truth, it worked and I'm doing great, but I still have my mishaps or moments of avoidance.

At the end of the day, we all have different attachment styles, and it's important to recognize that our own style may not fit everyone. The most important thing is to be aware of how your attachment style can manifest in your relationships, and strive for healthy connections every day. It's not easy, but it's worth the effort.

It's fascinating how we will neglect our own needs, fail to recognize our triggers, and struggle to understand our own emotions and behaviors. And without help, we will continue to remain a mystery to ourselves. So, my humble desire is that this book has provided you with enough solutions, self-awareness, and knowledge to finally begin to heal your wounds and improve your relationships for years to come.

And always remember that personal growth is a journey that never ends; take this book as your first step on the path to becoming the best version of yourself and continue to take small steps that allow you to be patient with the process. Now that you have a better understanding of your attachment style, go out there and start making secure connections today.

You got this!

*Elevate your journey with......*

# EXCLUSIVE COMPLIMENTARY
# SUPPORT MATERIALS!

## As a FREE Gift:

I have created a collection of **60+ journal pages and interactive worksheets** that perfectly complement the steps discussed in this book.

Simply go to:
## www.LeighWHart.com
to receive your FREE printable support materials.

# REFERENCES

*7 Tips For Changing Negative Behaviour*(n.d.). *Shift Collab.* https://www.
shiftcollab.com/blog/7-tips-for-changing-negative-behaviour

*5 Barriers to Behavior Change.* (n.d.). Td.org. https://www.td.org/insights/5-
barriers-to-behavior-change

*11 Signs of Secure Attachment in Adults.* (n.d.). Abundance No Limits. https://
www.abundancenolimits.com/signs-of-secure-attachment-in-adults/

*10 Ways To Set Boundaries With Difficult Family Members.* (2023, April 24).
Taylor Counseling Group. https://taylorcounselinggroup.com/blog/set-
boundaries-for-difficult-family-members/

*10 ways to practice self-acceptance.* (2023, January 13). Kids Help Phone. https://
kidshelpphone.ca/get-info/10-ways-practice-self-acceptance/

*10 Do's and Don'ts of Managing Relationship Expectations.* (n.d.). Relish. https://
hellorelish.com/articles/how-to-manage-expectations-in-a-
relationship.html

*50-inspiring-motivational-quotes-about-willpower-and-determination.html.* (n.d.).
Inc.com. https://www.inc.com/jeff-haden/50-inspiring-motivational-
quotes-about-willpower-and-determination.html

*50 Self-Affirmations to Help You Stay Motivated Every Day.* (2020, April 30). US
Oral Surgery Management. https://www.usosm.com/employee/50-self-
affirmations-to-help-you-stay-motivated-every-day/

*51 Self Care Quotes and Tiny Reminders to Love Yourself.* (n.d.). Fortune & Frame.
https://fortuneandframe.com/blogs/news/self-care-quotes

*77 reflection quotes for quiet moments.* (2023, February 15). TRVST. https://
www.trvst.world/environment/reflection-quotes/

*100 Relationship Quotes For Understanding Connection (2023).* (2021, September
14). YourFates. https://www.yourfates.com/relationship-quotes/

*A Big Ol' List Of Positive Affirmations To Use Any Time You Feel Down.* (2022,
August 4). Mindbodygreen. https://www.mindbodygreen.com/articles/
positive-affirmations

*A Brief Overview of Adult Attachment Theory and Research.* (n.d.). R. Chris Fraley.
http://labs.psychology.illinois.edu/~rcfraley/attachment.htm

Amft, T. B. (2023). *How Do I Know If My Mental Health Is Improving? Verywell Mind.* https://www.verywellmind.com/how-do-i-know-if-my-mental-health-is-improving-5199596

*Anxious Attachment in Relationships: 7 Ways To Support Your Partner.* (n.d.). Anti Loneliness. https://www.antiloneliness.com/relationships/how-to-support-an-anxiously-attached-partner

*Anxious Attachment Style in Relationships Complete Guide.* (2023, April 5). Attachment Project. https://www.attachmentproject.com/anxious-attachment-relationships/#:

Arabi, S., MA. (2017, August 21). *11 Signs Youre the Victim of Narcissistic Abuse.* Psych Central. https://psychcentral.com/blog/recovering-narcissist/2017/08/11-signs-youre-the-victim-of-narcissistic-abuse#1

*Attachment Style Quiz: Free & Fast Attachment Style Test.* (2022, November 18). Attachment Project. https://www.attachmentproject.com/attachment-style-quiz/

*Attachment theory | Features & Types.* (2016, August 30). Encyclopedia Britannica. https://www.britannica.com/science/attachment-theory/Individual-difference-features-of-attachment-theory

*Attachment Trauma.* (2023b). Choosing Therapy. https://www.choosingtherapy.com/attachment-trauma/

Avendaño, K. (2023, March 21). 45 Inspirational Mental Health Quotes That Are Supportive and Empowering. *Good Housekeeping.* https://www.goodhousekeeping.com/life/a39739060/mental-health-quotes/

*Avoidant attachment style - what's helped me and what I've been doing.* (2020, May 24). Beyond Blue Forums. https://forums.beyondblue.org.au/t5/relationship-and-family-issues/avoidant-attachment-style-what-s-helped-me-and-what-i-ve-been/td-p/442874

*Avoidant Attachment Style in Relationships - Complete Guide.* (2023, April 6). Attachment Project. https://www.attachmentproject.com/avoidant-attachment-relationships/

Awosika, T. (2023, February 14). The Dreadful 5: 5 Triggers for the Fearful Avoidant Attachment Style. *Medium.* https://medium.com/hello-love/the-dreadful-5-5-triggers-for-the-fearful-avoidant-attachment-style-1bffec57fa73

Baldwin, J. (2020, May 2). The Benefits of Writing Down Your Thoughts and Feelings - The Adroit Journal. *The Adroit Journal.* https://theadroitjournal.

org/2020/04/03/the-benefits-of-writing-down-your-thoughts-and-feelings/

Barkley, S. (2022, October 28). *Self Expectations: 7 Suggestions for Setting Realistic Expectations.* Psych Central. https://psychcentral.com/health/suggestions-for-setting-realistic-expectations-with-yourself

Barrell, A. (2020, June 2). *5 breathing exercises for anxiety and how to do them.* Medicalnewstoday . https://www.medicalnewstoday.com/articles/breathing-exercises-for-anxiety

BCom, M. R. (2023). *How to Be Mentally Strong: 14 Ways to Build Mental Toughness.* PositivePsychology.com. https://positivepsychology.com/mentally-strong/

Behavior pattern definition and meaning. (2023). In *Collins Dictionaries.* Collins English Dictionary. https://www.collinsdictionary.com/dictionary/english/behavior-pattern

*Benefits and Options for Therapy.* (2020, October 23). Healthline. https://www.healthline.com/health/benefits-of-therapy

*Bereavement During Childhood and Adolescence.* (1984). NCBI Bookshelf. https://www.ncbi.nlm.nih.gov/books/NBK217849/

Bijan. (2023, March 9). *13 Avoidant Attachment Triggers & How To Heal 2023. Coaching Online.* https://www.coaching-online.org/avoidant-attachment-triggers/

Bilge, I. S. (2023). *3 ways to support a partner with an anxious attachment style.* Rumie-learn. https://learn.rumie.org/jR/bytes/3-ways-to-support-a-partner-with-an-anxious-attachment-style

Blog, H. (2020). *How To Find Out Your Partner's Attachment Style.* Malminder Gill at Harley Street, London. https://www.hypnosis-in-london.com/how-to-find-out-your-partners-attachment-style/

Bretherton, I. (1992). The origns of attachment theory: John Bowlby and Mary Ainsworth. *APA PsycNet, 28(5), 759–775.* https://psycnet.apa.org/doi/10.1037/0012-1649.28.5.759

Brody, J. E. (2017, June 12). *Social Interaction Is Critical for Mental and Physical Health.* The New York Times. https://www.nytimes.com/2017/06/12/well/live/having-friends-is-good-for-you.html

Brown, J. (2022). *5 Big Relationship Expectations All Couples Need To Talk About.* Fatherly. https://www.fatherly.com/life/relationship-expectations-couples-need-to-discuss

*Calming the Anxious Attachment Style.* (2023, April 21). Happinessclinic. https://www.thehappinessclinic.org/single-post/calming-the-anxious-attachment-style

Canh. (2022). *Questions To Ask To Learn About Your Attachment Style.* Liberation Healing Seattle. https://www.liberationhealingseattle.com/blog-trauma-therapist/questions-to-ask-to-learn-about-your-upbringing-attachment-style

Cassata, C. (2021, September 25). *8 Ways to Accept Yourself.* Psych Central. https://psychcentral.com/lib/ways-to-accept-yourself

Ccs, H. S. M. L. L. (2023, April 7). *How to Set Boundaries With Friends (If You're Too Nice).* SocialSelf. https://socialself.com/blog/boundaries-friends/

Celina. (2022, May 24). *10 Things To Write In Your Journal Right Now.* Career Girl Daily. https://www.careergirldaily.com/10-things-to-write-in-your-journal-right-now/

Cherry, K. (2022). *The Different Types of Attachment Styles.* Verywell Mind. https://www.verywellmind.com/attachment-styles-2795344

Cherry, K. (2023a). *What Is Attachment Theory?* Verywell Mind. https://www.verywellmind.com/what-is-attachment-theory-2795337

Cherry, K. (2023b). *What Is Attachment Theory?* Verywell Mind. https://www.verywellmind.com/what-is-attachment-theory-2795337#toc-the-stages-of-attachment

*Child abuse - Symptoms and causes.* (2022, May 19). Mayo Clinic. https://www.mayoclinic.org/diseases-conditions/child-abuse/symptoms-causes/syc-20370864

*Child maltreatment.* (2022). World Health Organization. https://www.who.int/news-room/fact-sheets/detail/child-maltreatment

Co, P., & Co, P. (2021). *How a Parent's Affection Shapes a Child's Happiness for Life.* The Gottman Institute. https://www.gottman.com/blog/how-a-parents-affection-shapes-a-childs-happiness-for-life/#:

Cohut, M., PhD. (2018, February 23). *What are the health benefits of being social?* Medicalnewstoday.com. https://www.medicalnewstoday.com/articles/321019

*Consequences of Separation/Divorce for Children.* (2011, June 1). Encyclopedia on Early Childhood Development. https://www.child-encyclopedia.com/divorce-and-separation/according-experts/consequences-separationdivorce-children#:

Contributor, N. M. L. (2023). *Self Acceptance Quotes To Help You Find Inner Peace.* Everyday Power. https://everydaypower.com/quotes-on-acceptance-self-others/

Coronel, M. (n.d.). *Learn To Identify Behavior Patterns that are working against you at Work.* Linkedin.com. https://www.linkedin.com/pulse/learn-identify-behavior-patterns-working-against-you-work-coronel

Cuncic, A. (2022). *Effects of Narcissistic Abuse.* Verywell Mind. https://www.verywellmind.com/effects-of-narcissistic-abuse-5208164

David. (2022, September 20). *11 Anxious Attachment Triggers: Causes + How to Manage Them.* NCRW. https://ncrw.org/anxious-attachment-triggers/

Davis, S. (2021, February 25). *The Long-Term Effects of Abandonment.* CPTSDfoundation.org. https://cptsdfoundation.org/2021/02/25/the-long-term-effects-of-abandonment/

Dee. (2023). *17 Journaling Tips For Beginners (And How To Start).* Vanilla Papers. https://vanillapapers.net/2019/11/13/journaling-tips/

DiGiulio, S. (2021, October 6). *Self-Care: How to Do It Right Now.* EverydayHealth.com. https://www.everydayhealth.com/wellness/top-self-care-tips-for-being-stuck-at-home-during-the-coronavirus-pandemic/

DiSalvo, D. (2022, November 27). 8 Reasons Why Its so Hard to Really Change Your Behavior. *Psychology Today.* https://www.psychologytoday.com/us/blog/neuronarrative/201707/8-reasons-why-its-so-hard-really-change-your-behavior

*Domestic violence and abusive relationships.* (n.d.). Healthdirect Australia. https://www.healthdirect.gov.au/domestic-violence-and-abusive-relationships

*Daily Affirmations: Definition, Benefits, & 102 Examples to Improve Your Life.* (n.d.). The Berkeley Well-Being Institute. https://www.berkeleywellbeing.com/daily-affirmations.html

*Effects of child abuse and neglect for children and adolescents.* (n.d.). Australian Institute of Family Studies. https://aifs.gov.au/resources/policy-and-practice-papers/effects-child-abuse-and-neglect-children-and-adolescents

Engels, C. (2022). *12 surprising benefits of writing down your thoughts and feelings.* Ideapod. https://ideapod.com/6-surprising-benefits-writing-thoughts-feelings/

*Fearful Avoidant Attachment Triggers & How to Manage Them.* (2022, February 18). My AttachEd. https://myattached.com/2021/10/17/fearful-avoidant-attachment-triggers-how-to-manage-them/

Fedena. (2019, August 13). *How Poor Parental Support Affects Student Growth And Achievement?* Fedena Blog. https://fedena.com/blog/2019/07/how-poor-parental-support-affects-student-growth-and-achievement.html#:

Fellizar, K. (2018). *The Best Questions To Ask Yourself To Determine Which Of The 4 Attachment Styles You Are.* Bustle. https://www.bustle.com/p/the-best-questions-to-ask-yourself-to-determine-which-of-the-4-attachment-styles-you-are-9964503

Fiona. (2023a). *What are the different types of attachment?* The Wave Clinic. https://thewaveclinic.com/blog/what-are-the-different-types-of-attachment/

Fiona. (2023b). *What are the different types of attachment?* The Wave Clinic. https://thewaveclinic.com/blog/what-are-the-different-types-of-attachment/

Firestone, L., PhD. (2017, September 15). In a Relationship with a Narcissist? A Guide to Narcissistic Relationships. PsychAlive. https://www.psychalive.org/narcissistic-relationships/

Fletcher, J. (2022, August 16). *What are the effects of emotional abuse?* Medicalnewstoday. https://www.medicalnewstoday.com/articles/327080#long-term-effects

Fowler, P. (2018, January 11). *Breathing Techniques for Stress Relief.* WebMD. https://www.webmd.com/balance/stress-management/stress-relief-breathing-techniques

Fox, J. (2022). *How To Celebrate Small Wins And Make Greater Progress.* Feel More Connected. https://feelmoreconnected.com/how-to-celebrate-small-wins/

Gilmer, M. (2022, February 15). *How To Start a Self-Care Routine. Cleveland Clinic.* https://health.clevelandclinic.org/how-to-start-a-self-care-routine/

Gizzi, C. (2015, November 24). *18 Of The Most Powerful & Inspiring Quotes On Expectations.* Fearless Motivation. https://www.fearlessmotivation.com/2015/09/23/10-of-the-most-powerful-inspiring-quotes-on-expectations/

Glass, L. J. (2023). Opening Up Emotionally. *PIVOT.* https://www.lovetopivot.com/why-struggle-open-emotionally-important-relationship-intimacy-coaching/

Gotter, A. (2019, April 22). *8 Breathing Exercises to Try When You Feel Anxious.*

Healthline. https://www.healthline.com/health/breathing-exercises-for-anxiety

Grace, R. M. (2018, July 20). *3 signs of lack of affection in children.* Exploring Your Mind. https://exploringyourmind.com/3-signs-of-lack-of-affection-in-children/

Gupta, S. (2022). *How to Embrace Self-Acceptance.* Verywell Mind. https://www.verywellmind.com/self-acceptance-characteristics-importance-and-tips-for-improvement-6544468

Hadiah, & Hadiah. (2023). *Top 9 Avoidant Attachment Triggers (+7 Tips On Overcoming Avoidant Attachment Style).* Ineffable Living. https://ineffableliving.com/overcome-avoidant-attachment-style/

Hailey, L. (2022). *How to Set Boundaries: 5 Ways to Draw the Line Politely.* Science of People. https://www.scienceofpeople.com/how-to-set-boundaries/#:

Hayes, L. N. (n.d.). *6 Habits That Will Help You Build Mental Strength.* Shine. https://advice.theshineapp.com/articles/6-habits-that-will-help-you-build-mental-strength/

*Healing Trauma Quotes (79 quotes).* (n.d.). Goodreads. https://www.goodreads.com/quotes/tag/healing-trauma#:

*Health Benefits of Social Interaction.* (n.d.). Mercy Medical Center. https://www.mercycare.org/bhs/employee-assistance-program/eapforemployers/resources/health-benefits-of-social-interaction/#:

*Healthy Boundaries in Relationships: A Guide for Building and Keeping.* (n.d.). Betterup. https://www.betterup.com/blog/healthy-boundaries-in-relationships

Higgins, C. J. (2023, February 3). *How To Set Goals Together For A Healthier Relationship.* The Good Trade. https://www.thegoodtrade.com/features/couples-relationship-goals/

Holland, K. (2019, December 11). *How Fearful Avoidant Attachment Affects Relationships.* Healthline. https://www.healthline.com/health/mental-health/fearful-avoidant-attachment#signs

*How can I set boundaries with my family?* (2023, March 2). MHA Screening. https://screening.mhanational.org/content/how-can-i-set-boundaries-my-family/?layout=actions_neutral

*How to Break Bad Habits and Change Behaviors.* (2022, September 7). Heart.org.

https://www.heart.org/en/healthy-living/healthy-lifestyle/mental-health-and-wellbeing/how-to-break-bad-habits-and-change-behaviors

*How to change your mindset to achieve more in life with Tony.* (2021, November 2). Tonyrobbins.com. https://www.tonyrobbins.com/stories/coaching/changing-your-mindset/

*How to Change Your Mindset: 5 Ways to Change Your Mindset - 2023.* (2022, December 2). - MasterClass. https://www.masterclass.com/articles/how-to-change-your-mindset

*How to Cope with an Avoidant Partner.* (2022b, June 29). The School of Life. https://www.theschooloflife.com/article/how-to-cope-with-an-avoidant-partner//?/

How to Deal with Emotional Triggers. (2022). Kentucky Counseling Center. https://kentuckycounselingcenter.com/how-to-deal-with-emotional-triggers/

*How to say no to others (and why you shouldn't feel guilty).* (n.d.). Betterup. https://www.betterup.com/blog/how-to-say-no

*How to set boundaries with emotionally draining friends.* (n.d.). Happiful Magazine. https://happiful.com/how-to-set-boundaries-with-emotionally-draining-friends/

*How to Start Journaling and Stick to It [The Ultimate Guide].* (2022, July 7). Develop Good Habits. https://www.developgoodhabits.com/start-journaling/

Hugo. (2023). *7 Things to Write in Your Journal (For Positivity and Growth).* Tracking Happiness. https://www.trackinghappiness.com/what-to-write-in-your-journal/

Hutto, C. (2020). *14 Creative Ways to Celebrate Small Wins.* InHerSight. https://www.inhersight.com/blog/career-development/celebrate-small-wins

*If You're Kind Of Afraid Of Relationships, This Might Be Your Attachment Style.* (2023, March 23). Mindbodygreen. https://www.mindbodygreen.com/articles/how-fearful-avoidant-attachment-style-affects-your-sex-life

*In Longest and Most Detailed Study of Pediatric Grief Following Parental Loss to Date, Department Researchers Find Increased Rates of Depression and Functional Impairment.* (2018, November 16). University of Pittsburgh Department of Psychiatry. https://www.psychiatry.pitt.edu/news/longest-and-most-detailed-study-pediatric-grief-following-parental-loss-date-department#:

Indeed Editorial Team. (2022). *How To Measure Your Progress Effectively in 5*

*Steps.* Indeed Career Guide. https://www.indeed.com/career-advice/career-development/measure-progress#:

Ishak, R. (2015). *6 Ways To Be More Open With Your Partner.* Bustle. https://www.bustle.com/articles/128557-6-ways-to-be-more-open-with-your-partner

James, S. (2020, October 4). *3 Easy Steps To Change Any Negative Behaviour Or Emotional State.* Project Life Mastery. https://projectlifemastery.com/3-easy-steps-to-change-any-negative-behaviour-or-emotional-state/

Johnston, C. (2022). *51 Self Care Ideas To Kickstart Your Self Care Routine.* Wholefully. https://wholefully.com/self-care-ideas/

Jones, R. (2023). *75 Boundaries Quotes About Setting Limits in Your Relationships.* Happier Human. https://www.happierhuman.com/boundaries-quotes/

*Journaling for Mental Health.* (n.d.). University of Rochester Medical Center. https://www.urmc.rochester.edu/encyclopedia/content.aspx?ContentID=4552&ContentTypeID=1#:

Kogan, V. (2021, April 22). *Boost Your Self-Confidence With Self-Acknowledgement.* Forbes. https://www.forbes.com/sites/forbescoachescouncil/2021/04/22/boost-your-self-confidence-with-self-acknowledgement/?sh=492779991319

Krstic, Z., & Dolgoff, S. (2023, January 9). *50 Best Self-Care Ideas for Mental and Physical Wellbeing.* Good Housekeeping. https://www.goodhousekeeping.com/health/wellness/g25643343/self-care-ideas/

Laderer, A., Mutziger, J., Laderer, A., & Mutziger, J. (2023). *10 goals you can set to strengthen your relationship in 2023, according to couples therapists.* Insider. https://www.insider.com/guides/health/sex-relationships/relationship-goals

Lawler, M. (2022, August 26). How to Start a Self-Care Routine You'll Follow. EverydayHealth.com. https://www.everydayhealth.com/self-care/start-a-self-care-routine/

Lawler, M. (2023, March 17). What Is Self-Care, and Why Is It So Important for Your Health? EverydayHealth.com. https://www.everydayhealth.com/self-care/

Lcpc, S. a. M. (2023). *9 Breathing Exercises to Relieve Anxiety.* Verywell Mind. https://www.verywellmind.com/abdominal-breathing-2584115

Lcsw, A. M. (2022). *The Psychological Effects of Divorce on Children.* Verywell

Family. https://www.verywellfamily.com/psychological-effects-of-divorce-on-kids-4140170

Lcsw, K. S., DD. (2022). *How to Set Healthy Boundaries With Friends.* Talkspace. https://www.talkspace.com/blog/friendship-boundaries/

*Learn How to Start Journaling. It's a Ritual Worth the Time.* (n.d.). Betterup. https://www.betterup.com/blog/how-to-start-journaling

*Learning How To Open Up To People.* (n.d.). BetterHelp. https://www.betterhelp.com/advice/how-to/learning-how-to-open-up-to-people/

Lebow, H. I. (2022a, June 22). *Anxious Attachment Style: Signs, Causes, and How to Change.* Psych Central. https://psychcentral.com/health/anxious-attachment-style-signs

Lebow, H. I. (2022b, July 5). *How to Increase Intimacy and Communication with an Avoidant Partner: 21 Ways.* Psych Central. https://psychcentral.com/relationships/ways-to-increase-intimacy-and-communication-with-an-avoidant-partner

Levitan, H. (2022, July 13). *What Is Fearful Avoidant Attachment Style, And How Does It Impact Relationships?* Women's Health. https://www.womenshealthmag.com/relationships/a40383169/fearful-attachment-style/

Li, P. (2023). *How Does The Death Of A Parent Affect A Child.* Parenting for Brain. https://www.parentingforbrain.com/death-of-a-parent/

Lippold, M. A., Davis, K. C., Lawson, K. M., & McHale, S. M. (2016). Day-to-day Consistency in Positive Parent–Child Interactions and Youth Well-Being. *Journal of Child and Family Studies, 25*(12), 3584–3592. https://doi.org/10.1007/s10826-016-0502-x

Madeson, M., PhD. (2023). *The Importance of Counseling: 14 Proven Benefits of Therapy.* PositivePsychology.com. https://positivepsychology.com/why-counseling-is-important/

Manson, M. (2023, February 8). *The Guide to Strong Relationship Boundaries.* Mark Manson. https://markmanson.net/boundaries

Marcin, A. (2020, May 7). *10 Effects of Divorce on Children — and Helping Them Cope.* Healthline. https://www.healthline.com/health/parenting/effects-of-divorce-on-children

Martin, S. (2021a). *6 Benefits of Setting Boundaries.* Live Well With Sharon Martin. https://www.livewellwithsharonmartin.com/6-benefits-of-setting-boundaries/

Martin, S. (2021b). *Healing the Psychological Effects of Abandonment.* Live Well

With Sharon Martin. https://www.livewellwithsharonmartin.com/heal ing-psychological-effects-of-abandonment/#:

MbBCh, S. A. (2021, July 1). *The Importance Of Setting Healthy Boundaries.* Forbes. https://www.forbes.com/sites/forbescoachescouncil/2021/07/01/the-importance-of-setting-healthy-boundaries/?sh=740bae0356e4

Mcleod, S., PhD. (2023). *Attachment Theory.* Simply Psychology. https://www.simplypsychology.org/attachment.html

Meah, A., & Meah, A. (2017). *30 Inspirational Quotes On Attachment.* Awaken-TheGreatnessWithin. https://www.awakenthegreatnesswithin.com/30-inspirational-quotes-on-attachment/

Medcalf, A. (2023, February 16). *The Truth About Setting Relationship Goals.* Abby Medcalf. https://abbymedcalf.com/the-truth-about-setting-relationship-goals/

Meyer, A. (n.d.). *Here's How to Actually Make Journaling a Habit.* Shine. https://advice.theshineapp.com/articles/heres-how-to-actually-make-journaling-a-habit/

Miller-Wilson, K. (2020). *100+ Relationship Goals Quotes to Motivate and Inspire.* LoveToKnow. https://dating.lovetoknow.com/helpful-dating-resources/100-relationship-goals-quotes-motivate-inspire

Milton, R. S. &. J. (2023). *This 5min Relationship Check In Will Transform Your Marriage.* Practical Intimacy. https://practicalintimacy.com/relationship-check-in/

Ministerie van Justitie en Veiligheid. (2016, February 4). *What happens to the responsibility for my children if I get divorced?* Government.nl. https://www.government.nl/topics/family-law/question-and-answer/responsibility-for-my-children-if-i-get-divorced

Minutillo, M. (2019, April 25). *It's Okay To Have Expectations For People.* Thought Catalog. https://thoughtcatalog.com/megan-minutillo/2019/04/its-okay-to-have-expectations-for-people/

Morales-Brown, L. (2020a, October 30). *Attachment disorder in adults: What is it?* Medicalnewstoday. https://www.medicalnewstoday.com/articles/attachment-disorder-in-adults#relationships

Morales-Brown, L. (2020b, October 30). *Attachment disorder in adults: What is it?* Medicalnewstoday. https://www.medicalnewstoday.com/articles/attachment-disorder-in-adults#types-of-the-disorder

Ms, M. T. (2021, June 14). *How and When to Say No.* Psych Central. https://

psychcentral.com/lib/learning-to-say-no

*Narcissistic Abuse.* (2023a). Choosing Therapy. https://www.choosingtherapy. com/narcissistic-abuse/

Ncsp, J. H. P. B. (2022, July 26). *Importance of a Support System.* Highland Springs. https://highlandspringsclinic.org/the-benefits-and-importance-of-a-support-system/

Nurse, R. (n.d.). *The Power of Self-Acknowledgement.* Utahbariatrics. https:// utahbariatrics.com/the-power-of-self-acknowledgement/

Ontheroadagain. (2020, November 3). *Anxious attachment and relationships - help! [Online forum post].* Mental Health Forum. https://www.mentalhealth forum.net/forum/threads/anxious-attachment-and-relationships-help. 245992/

*Opening Up Quotes (26 quotes).* (n.d.). Goodreads. https://www.goodreads.com/ quotes/tag/opening-up

Orloff, J., MD. (2021, April 22). *5 Techniques to Heal Your Emotional Triggers.* Psychology Today. https://www.psychologytoday.com/us/blog/the-empaths-survival-guide/201902/5-techniques-heal-your-emotional-triggers

Parvez, H. (2022, October 21). *Avoidant attachment triggers to be aware of.* PsychMechanics. https://www.psychmechanics.com/avoidant-attach ment-triggers/

Pattemore, C. (2021, June 4). *How to Set Boundaries in Your Relationships.* Psych Central. https://psychcentral.com/blog/why-healthy-relationships-always-have-boundaries-how-to-set-boundaries-in-yours

*Pattern of Behavior Definition.* (n.d.). Law Insider. https://www.lawinsider. com/dictionary/pattern-of-behavior

*Pattern Of Behavior Quotes (4 quotes).* (n.d.). Goodreads. https://www. goodreads.com/quotes/tag/pattern-of-behavior

Paulahurd. (2020). *How to Recognize Repetitive Patterns of Thought, Emotion, and Behavior.* Wholebeing Institute. https://wholebeinginstitute.com/recog nize-repetitive-patterns/

Perera BA, MA, DipLC, K., & DipLC, K. P. B. M. (2022). *The Importance of Self Acceptance.* More Self Esteem. https://more-selfesteem.com/more-self-esteem/building-self-esteem/the-significance-of-self-acceptance/

Petersen, A. C. (2014, March 25). *Consequences of Child Abuse and Neglect.* NCBI Bookshelf. https://www.ncbi.nlm.nih.gov/books/NBK195987/

Plumptre, E. (2021). *Mental Health Effects of Different Types of Abuse.* Verywell Mind. https://www.verywellmind.com/how-does-abuse-affect-mental-health-5203897

PSYCH Authority. (2023a, January 25). *10 Signs of Anxious Attachment Style in Relationships (Attachment Theory)* [Video]. YouTube. https://www.youtube.com/watch?v=oz3VdgZqpno

PSYCH Authority. (2023b, January 28). *10 Signs of Secure Attachment Style in Relationships (Attachment Theory)* [Video]. YouTube. https://www.youtube.com/watch?v=uQ1-APAhOHA

PSYCH Authority. (2023c, January 30). *10 Signs of Fearful-Avoidant Attachment Style in Relationships (Disorganized)* [Video]. YouTube. https://www.youtube.com/watch?v=A5gPisklpkY

Psych2Go. (2020a, June 30). *8 Signs of an Avoidant Attachment Style* [Video]. YouTube. https://www.youtube.com/watch?v=nqlce10FyVU

Psych2Go. (2020b, December 21). *8 Signs of an Anxious Attachment Style* [Video]. YouTube. https://www.youtube.com/watch?v=g-466psrXrA

*Realistic Expectations.* (2020, November 10). Workforce Wellness. https://www.vdh.virginia.gov/workforce-wellness/realistic-expectations/

Ricki. (2015, February 15). *Decoding Your Partner's Attachment Style - The Love Compass.* The Love Compass. https://the-love-compass.com/2014/02/14/decoding-your-partners-attachment-style/

Rrt, J. L. B. (2023). 99+ Best Quotes About Breathing (Respiratory Edition). *Respiratory Therapy Zone.* https://www.respiratorytherapyzone.com/quotes-about-breathing/

Ryan Liberty / Mental Health. (2018, November 2). *Examples of Avoidant Attachment in Relationships* [Video]. YouTube. https://www.youtube.com/watch?v=AFjek4ZE0io

Ryder, G. (2022, January 19). *What Is Attachment Trauma?* Psych Central. https://psychcentral.com/health/attachment-trauma#causes

Sanchez, M. (2022). *How to Manage Expectations in a Relationship.* Sesh. https://www.seshgroups.com/blog/how-to-manage-expectations-in-a-relationship

Schneider, K. (2022, December 9). *How To Build Mental Strength and Toughness.* Cleveland Clinic. https://health.clevelandclinic.org/mental-strength/

Scott, S. (2023). *What to Write About in a Journal: 59 Journaling Ideas.* Develop Good Habits. https://www.developgoodhabits.com/what-write-journal/

*Seeking Help for Your Mental Health Is Brave. And Beneficial.* (n.d.). Betterup. https://www.betterup.com/blog/seeking-help

Seip, J. (2022). *How To Self-Soothe and Heal Anxious Attachment.* Be Well Therapy Group. https://bewelltherapygroup.org/2022/02/22/how-to-self-soothe-and-heal-anxious-attachment/

Seiter, C., & Seiter, C. (2022). *The Complete Guide To Fearful Avoidant Triggers.* Ex Boyfriend Recovery. https://www.exboyfriendrecovery.com/the-fearful-avoidant-triggers/

Seppälä, E. (2021, September 17). *Research: Why Breathing Is So Effective at Reducing Stress.* Harvard Business Review. https://hbr.org/2020/09/research-why-breathing-is-so-effective-at-reducing-stress

*Setting Boundaries.* (2021, March 26). WebMD. https://www.webmd.com/mental-health/setting-boundaries

Sevenmindsets. (2022). *How to Change Your Mindset.* 7 Mindsets. https://7mindsets.com/how-to-change-your-mindset/

Sharma, S. (2022, November 18). *Want To Set Realistic Expectations For Yourself? Try These 7 Ways!* Calm Sage. https://www.calmsage.com/how-to-set-realistic-expectations-for-yourself/

Sherman, A., PhD. (2017, July 22). *19 Lasting Effects of Abandoning or Emotionally Unavailable Parents.* Psych Central. https://psychcentral.com/blog/dysfunction/2017/07/19-lasting-effects-of-abandoning-or-emotionally-unavailable-parents#1

Smith, M. (2018, December 22). *Consequences of a Lack of Affection in Childhood.* You Are Mom. https://youaremom.com/children/lack-of-affection-in-childhood/

Smith, M., MA. (2023). *Setting Healthy Boundaries in Relationships.* HelpGuide.org. https://www.helpguide.org/articles/relationships-communication/setting-healthy-boundaries-in-relationships.htm

Smith, S., & Smith, S. (2021, August 31). *35 Relationship Goals.* Marriage Advice. https://www.marriage.com/advice/relationship/realistic-relationship-goals/

Soman, P. (2023). *4 Sure-Shot Steps To Suppress Negative Thoughts.* ThinkRight.me. https://www.thinkrightme.com/how-to-change-your-behaviour-from-negative-to-positive/

Staff, G. (2022). Why Setting Relationship Goals Is Important And How to Do It. Goalcast. https://www.goalcast.com/setting-relationship-goals/

Staff, M. (2013). *Working Together: The Importance of Consistency in Parenting.* Melbourne Child Psychology. https://www.melbournechildpsychology. com.au/blog/working-together-the-importance-of-consistency-in-parenting/#:

Staff. (n.d.). *8 Simple Tips on How to Celebrate Small Wins Daily.* Great Performers Academy. https://greatperformersacademy.com/motivation/ 8-simple-tips-on-how-to-celebrate-small-wins-daily

*Talking about your mental health problem.* (n.d.). Mind. https://www.mind.org. uk/information-support/guides-to-support-and-services/seeking-help-for-a-mental-health-problem/talking-to-friends-family/

Tanasugarn, A., PhD. (2022, May 5). *How Childhood Attachment Trauma Can Affect Adult Relationships.* Psychology Today. https://www.psychologyto day.com/intl/blog/understanding-ptsd/202205/how-childhood-attach ment-trauma-can-affect-adult-relationships

Team, C. (2021). How do breathing exercises reduce stress? | Calmer. *Calmer.* https://www.thisiscalmer.com/blog/how-do-breathing-exercises-allevi ate-stress#:

Team, O. (2021, October 11). *64 Bad Behavior Quotes.* OverallMotivation. https://www.overallmotivation.com/quotes/bad-behavior-quotes/

Team. (2022a, July 15). *Avoidant Attachment Triggers - Tips and Guide.* Attachment Project. https://www.attachmentproject.com/blog/avoidant-attachment-triggers/

Team. (2022b, December 18). *How to Communicate With an Avoidant Partner.* Attachment Project. https://www.attachmentproject.com/blog/communi cate-with-avoidant-partner/#:

Team. (2023a, April 5). *Self Regulation Strategies for Anxious Attachment Triggers.* Attachment Project. https://www.attachmentproject.com/blog/self-regula tion-anxious-attachment-triggers/

Team. (2023b, April 6). *Attachment Styles and Their Role in Adult Relationships.* Attachment Project. https://www.attachmentproject.com/blog/four-attachment-styles/

Team. (2023c, April 6). *Self-Regulation Tips for Disorganized Attachment Style Triggers.* Attachment Project. https://www.attachmentproject.com/blog/ self-regulation-disorganized-attachment-triggers/

Tewari, A. (2022). *60 Healing Quotes to Help You Recover From Hurt and Pain.* Gratitude - the Life Blog. https://blog.gratefulness.me/healing-quotes/

Thalia. (2023). *How To Build a Quick and Simple Self-Care Routine For Every Day of the Week*. Notes by Thalia. https://notesbythalia.com/build-a-simple-self-care-routine/

*The 17 Best Quotes about attachment*. (n.d.). Bookroo. https://bookroo.com/quotes/attachment

The Attachment Style Questionnaire. (2022a, March 17). *The School Of Life*. https://www.theschooloflife.com/article/the-attachment-style-questionnaire/

The Importance of Goal Setting in Relationships. (2022, June 17). Coblossomapp. https://www.coblossom.com/post/the-importance-of-goal-setting-in-relationships

*The importance of self care*. (n.d.). Perimeterhealthcare. https://www.perimeterhealthcare.com/news/posts/the-importance-of-self-care

*The Importance of Self-care*. (2022, November 3). #BeThe1To. https://www.bethe1to.com/the-importance-of-self-care/

*The Importance of Setting Boundaries: 10 Benefits for You and Your Relationships*. (n.d.). BetterHelp. https://www.betterhelp.com/advice/general/the-importance-of-setting-boundaries-10-benefits-for-you-and-your-relationships/

*The Only 2 Things You Need to Know to Change Negative Behaviors for Good*. (n.d.). Happify.com. https://www.happify.com/hd/2-things-to-change-negative-behaviors-for-good/

*The Path to Self-Acceptance*. (n.d.). Betterup. https://www.betterup.com/blog/self-acceptance#:

The Personal Development School. (2022, December 3). *Top 10 Signs You Have A Fearful Avoidant Attachment Style AKA Disorganized Attachment Style* [Video]. YouTube. https://www.youtube.com/watch?v=5Yjxjp4VvL8

The power of consistency while parenting young children. (2023, April 5). Sanford Health News. https://news.sanfordhealth.org/parenting/the-power-of-consistency/#:

The Proem Behavioral Health Team. (2023, January 24). How to Measure Progress Toward Mental Health Outcomes. Proem Health. https://blog.proemhealth.com/how-to-measure-progress-toward-mental-health-outcomes

Thompson, R. (2021, December 16). *The Importance of Writing Your Thoughts Down - The Ninja Writers Pub*. Medium. https://medium.com/ninja-writers/the-importance-of-writing-your-thoughts-down-f1b61cdfb117

*To Love Is To Be Vulnerable: How To Open Up.* (n.d.). *BetterHelp.* https://www. betterhelp.com/advice/love/to-love-is-to-be-vulnerable-how-to-open-up/

Torres, E. (2023, April 25). *99 Positive Morning Affirmations You Can Use Daily.* The Good Trade. https://www.thegoodtrade.com/features/positive-affir mations-morning-routine/

Tracy, U. M. (2022, March 5). The trauma of commission and omission. Medium. https://uncontrollablyme.medium.com/the-trauma-of-commis sion-and-omission-69f40f9f170f

*Trauma Through Omission.* (2021, May 24). Jennifer Nurick. https:// jennynurick.com/trauma-through-omission/

*Traumas of Commission.* (2020, August 26). Complex Trauma Resources. https://www.complextrauma.org/glossary/traumas-of-comission/

*Traumas of Omission.* (2019, February 24). Complex Trauma Resources. https://www.complextrauma.org/glossary/traumas-of-omission/

ValiantDetox. (2023, April 17). *How Do I Set Realistic Expectations?* Valiant Living Detox and Assessment. https://www.valiantdetox.com/how-do-i-set-realistic-expectations/

Villines, Z. (2023, January 11). *What to know about abandonment issues.* Medicalnewstoday. https://www.medicalnewstoday.com/articles/aban donment-issues

Ward, C. (2022, March 18). *Attachment Style Quiz.* Psych Central. https://psych central.com/quizzes/attachment-style-quiz

Weaver, J. (2020). *30+ Inspirational Quotes About Journaling.* But First, Joy. https://butfirstjoy.com/30-inspirational-quotes-about-journaling/

WebMD Editorial Contributors. (2021, March 11). *What Is Avoidant Attachment?* WebMD. https://www.webmd.com/parenting/what-is-avoidant-attachment

Weingus, L. (2021). *Here's Exactly How to Make Journaling a Habit.* Silk + Sonder. https://www.silkandsonder.com/blogs/news/heres-exactly-how-to-make-journaling-a-habit

*What Are the Effects of Divorce on Children?* (n.d.). FamilyMeans. https://www. familymeans.org/effects-of-divorce-on-children.html

*What is Mental Strength? 7 Ways to Develop More Than Mental Toughness.* (n.d.). Betterup. https://www.betterup.com/blog/mental-strength

*What is Self-Care and Why is it Important For You?* (2020, April 14). SNHU.

https://www.snhu.edu/about-us/newsroom/health/what-is-self-care

*Why it's Good to Have Expectations in Your Relationship.* (2021, April 2). Prepare/Enrich. https://www.prepare-enrich.com/blog/why-its-good-to-have-expectations-in-your-relationship/#:

*Why Setting Couple Goals Is Important For A Healthy Relationship.* (n.d.). ReGain. https://www.regain.us/advice/general/why-setting-couple-goals-is-important-for-a-healthy-relationship/

Williams, F. (2022, October 28). *What to know about fearful avoidant attachments.* Medicalnewstoday. https://www.medicalnewstoday.com/articles/fearful-avoidant-attachments

Williams, V. (2022). *Mayo Clinic Minute: The benefits of being socially connected.* News Network. https://newsnetwork.mayoclinic.org/discussion/mayo-clinic-minute-the-benefits-of-being-socially-connected/

Yoho. (2021). *What Are the Benefits of Seeking Professional Counseling?* Emerald Psychiatry & TMS Center. https://emeraldpsychiatry.com/what-are-the-benefits-of-seeking-professional-counseling/

Yuko, E. (2023, March 1). *This Is What It Looks Like to Set Healthy Boundaries.* Real Simple. https://www.realsimple.com/health/mind-mood/emotional-health/how-to-set-boundaries

Zola, M. (2021). *How to Set Healthy Boundaries in Your Relationship.* Eugene Therapy. https://eugenetherapy.com/article/how-to-set-healthy-boundaries-in-your-relationship/

Zwart, H. (n.d.). *Benefits of Writing Your Thoughts.* BetterYou. https://www.betteryou.ai/benefits-of-writing-your-thoughts/

Made in United States
Troutdale, OR
02/09/2024